Never a Hero
to Me

Never a Hero to Me

TRACY BLACK

SIMON &
SCHUSTER

London · New York · Sydney · Toronto

A CBS COMPANY

First published in Great Britain by Simon & Schuster UK Ltd, 2011
A CBS COMPANY

3 5 7 9 10 8 6 4

Simon & Schuster UK Ltd
1st Floor
222 Gray's Inn Road
London WC1X 8HB

www.simonandschuster.co.uk

Simon & Schuster Australia
Sydney

A CIP catalogue record for this book is available
from the British Library.

ISBN: 978-0-85720-329-8

Typeset by M Rules
Printed in the UK by CPI Cox & Wyman, Reading Berkshire RG1 8EX

For my partner, who is also my friend and soulmate. His belief in me has never wavered, his love for me remains strong, and his support for me in my darkest moments gave me strength.

For my children who, unknowingly, taught me that a mother's love for her children is unconditional. Through hard times we have always been there for each other – they make me proud to be a loving mum.

And for those brave, good men and women in the armed forces, the ones who protect and serve us – there are plenty of them.

CONTENTS

PROLOGUE

HEROES

My story is a normal one. Horrific and normal.

I was a normal little girl in a normal little family. There was me and my big brother, Gary. There was my mum, Valerie, and there was my dad, Harry. We were a perfect nuclear family on the surface – and a completely dysfunctional, abusive one underneath. For years, no one bothered to scratch that surface, no one bothered to ask one of a thousand questions which could have blown the whole thing apart.

For years, I kept it inside. I blamed myself for what my dad did to me. I blamed myself for not being stronger or louder. I even blamed myself for not being a better little girl, because I must have been bad for him to do what he did. But the truth was, the stories he managed to weave around me, the detailed lies he managed to spin, were so believable that I actually ended up believing I 'had' to do the things he forced upon me.

My father was held in high esteem. But it was all a front.

He was a bully. He was a child-beater. He was a paedophile. As a soldier, he was seen as a hero by many. But he was never a hero to me.

I'm a grown woman in her forties. I'm a mother and a grandmother, I have a life in the sun and a loving man by my side, but I also have many ghosts which have lingered for too many years. This is my story. I've needed to tell it for such a very long time – and, at last, in doing so I can claim back everything he took from me. I know I'm not the only child who suffered these horrors, but if in writing this I can reach out to even one person and tell them what I've learned, it will be worth it. It is *never* the child's fault. There is nothing you can do that makes abuse something you deserve. What you do deserve is freedom from the torment you have carried all these years, forgiveness from yourself and a realisation that you are more than what was done to you.

There may be scars, there may be pain. There may be memories which rear their heads every day. But you got through it. Some days, it may not feel that way, but there is always hope and there is always tomorrow. Those of us who survived? We're the invisible heroes – no one will ever give us a medal for what we endured in those dark days when we thought the hurting would never end, but we got through. We're the heroes.

FOREWORD

Tracy Black has wanted to tell her story of horror and survival for many years. Terrified that no one would believe her, one day she made a promise to the little girl she had been – she would tell the world what that child had endured, no matter how hard it would be to revisit her past. Now in her forties, Tracy lives in Europe with her partner and is a successful businesswoman. A mother of two, she has fought through her childhood and domestic abuse, and recently graduated from university with undergraduate and postgraduate degrees. She plans to undertake further study in the near future and will always fight for the victims of paedophiles. Tracy Black is a pseudonym. Names have been changed to protect anonymity.

CHAPTER 1

I WANT MY MUM

Rinteln, Germany, 1967

I looked out of the lounge window, fascinated by the torrential and persistent rain battering the glass. I was feeling pleased with myself, proud that I was tackling my homework easily and quickly despite being at my new school for only three weeks. At five years of age, in a strange country with many people speaking a language I could understand only a few words of, the Army school was a welcome haven for me. I had been in school for a little while in Singapore, but had never been such a big girl that I was given homework. It felt terribly grown-up to bring home my tiny satchel with a reading book, writing jotter and a note saying what I needed to do for the next day.

The house we lived in wasn't particularly homely – Army accommodation never was – but in my bedroom I had my few toys, my beloved golliwog and some books. I didn't want to be in there at that moment though. I had homework to do, and I needed an audience for that as much as anything. I wanted my family to see how grown-up I was with reading to do and numbers to learn. I had my family around me, and I was so sure that I would make friends and have a lovely time there. I had a simple, childlike belief that everything was coming together for me; little did I know how quickly it could all fall apart.

My dad had been in the Army since before I was born and I didn't know any other life. We were in Germany, but the camp was like a little Britain, isolated from local culture and local life, a version of home even though it was hundreds of miles away. I was born on a different Army base in 1962, and we stayed there for a couple of years before going to Germany. After that, we went to Singapore, but I remember very little of my first four or five years; nothing more than snippets really. We were never settled, it could change at any point, but that was just life. As a child, you absorb so much of what has gone on in the past, of what your parents' lives have been like, of what their expectations are, without ever being explicitly told. I assumed my dad had an important job, which meant we often had to move about. I knew this had 'always' been the case (in my mind, 'always' wasn't a concept that made much sense – at five years old the time between one birthday and the next seemed to take forever) and it was just the way things were. All around me, other children were living the same lives in anonymous houses with a determination not to put down roots, but school was making everything seem much more settled, much more permanent.

I had spent so much time looking forward to attending

classes. All summer I had been counting down the days, asking my mum how many sleeps it would be until I was there. She was exasperated (or perhaps just bored) with my constant enthusiasm, but I was thrilled that every day was a step closer. I would look at my school bag every night before I went to bed, line my shoes up neatly for the hundredth time, and dream about the wonderful time I would have.

For the first two days of my life as a schoolgirl, Mum had taken me and my big brother Gary to class in the morning. The school I was now at, my very first big-girl school, was near to the living quarters and, after those first mornings, she decided it was safe enough for us to go alone. She wasn't wrong in that sense – for children, Army bases are probably one of the most secure environments they could ever be in. I didn't have the slightest inkling at that stage of where danger would really lie, or of how close to home it would be. I would have liked Mum to have kept taking me to school for a little longer, but she told me that I was a big girl now – which I always liked to hear – and I didn't need her. That didn't feel quite right, I did need her, but she wasn't the sort of warm, cuddly mummy I saw with other kids at the school gate, so I wasn't too surprised when she stopped taking me there so quickly.

She passed the responsibility over to Gary, who was a few years older than me. He wasn't exactly delighted to be in charge of his little sister, but he had no choice in the matter and, for the next few days, took me on his own. I didn't like that, for he used our time together to nip my arms, pull my hair and push me into puddles. I soon realised he was only doing this to show off in front of the boys he hoped would be his friends, but I hated it and needed it to stop. I had made friends quickly and knew some of the other girls walked to school on their own. After my first week, I collared Mum in the kitchen one night to test the waters.

'Mum?' I began.

'What now?' she sighed, continuing to peel potatoes for dinner.

'I'm a big girl now, aren't I?'

'Why? What do you want?' she asked, narrowing her eyes at me as she turned round.

'Well, Sophie and Debbie in my class don't have big brothers ... and they get to walk to school on their own.'

'So?' she queried, concentrating on the potatoes again now that she knew I wasn't after anything that would cost money or time.

'So, can I walk to school on my own? I'd be good. I'd be careful. I promise. Please, Mum? Please?' I begged.

I was putting in more effort than required.

'Do what you like,' she muttered.

I was delighted that I had managed to get Mum to agree that I could go with the others, as it served the dual purpose of getting Gary away from me and making me feel even more grown up. I wasn't too bothered by the fact that she didn't seem particularly interested in what I did because, just as I accepted we might move at any time, I also accepted that my mum wasn't the most loving person in the world. Of course, I would have preferred things to be different, but I was well aware that she had other things on her mind. The thing was, Mum wasn't very well. I had no idea what was actually wrong with her, but I wasn't the only one – I knew from listening to snippets of her conversations with Dad when she came back from the medical centre that the doctors were clueless too. She was often sick and I would hear her vomiting at all times of the day and night. Sometimes the sound would wake me up as it was so loud and she would moan in pain when it happened.

I had also seen these weird lumpy things on her body, like boils, and knew her skin hurt a lot of the time. She would rub horrible smelly stuff into it that she told me was paraffin oil, and the stench of it filled our house. When she was unwell, she would tell me she couldn't be bothered with me, and Dad would say that I had to leave her alone, so I knew she might be in pain or feeling unwell when I asked her about walking to school on my own. Maybe that was why she had seemed so disinterested.

Whatever the reason, by the time I was sitting at the table, with my books and jotter in front of me, I was glad I had been allowed to walk to school with Debbie and the others, because it was all part of becoming grown up. Gary wasn't able to get at me when I was with other people and, to be honest, he wasn't that bothered anyway, as he could go off with his friends now he no longer had to take care of me.

I was concentrating so hard on my work that my tongue was poking out between my lips and my eyes were screwed up – I couldn't really read yet and numbers were still a bit tricky, but I was determined to try really hard. I got distracted by the weather and, as I watched the rain pour down the window, all these changes were floating around in my head, making me feel so happy – until I heard Gary guffawing over my shoulder. Quickly, my thoughts were dragged from how proud I would be to hand in my work to a sense that my brother knew something I didn't.

'What is it, Gary?' I asked. 'Why are you laughing at me?'

He snatched my homework book from my lap and sniggered. 'You're stupid! Anybody would laugh when they saw how stupid you were.' He waved the notebook around in front of me, dangling it in front of my face as he ridiculed me. 'You don't know how to use capital letters or anything – the only thing you've got right is your name. And that's stupid, just like you.' I looked over to Dad, sitting in front of the telly, oblivious to everything that was going on. I knew he wouldn't intervene, but I didn't want him to anyway; he wasn't the parent I needed. With tears welling in my eyes, I snatched my book back from Gary and rushed to find Mum.

I'd tell on him. I'd tell her how awful he was to me, and she'd sort him out. I knew she was in her bedroom, so I rushed there from the lounge, full of hot tears at how Gary had spoken to me, with an urgent need for Mum to make it all right. I barged in, the words all ready to tumble out – and froze. My mother was bent in half over a basin, vomiting violently. Her body was convulsing in pain and the sickness was coming fast. As always, I had no idea what was wrong with her, but knew she was so ill she was in no state to deal with my childish disputes. She looked up weakly, but had neither the strength nor the ability to even talk to me, promptly bending over the basin again and retching once more.

I backed out of the room, full of concern for her, but also worried. This had happened so many times before, but there seemed to be a violence to the sickness now that I hadn't been aware of previously. Mum had been taken ill the week before and, as young as I was, even I couldn't help but notice that she seemed to be getting worse as time went on. Ordinarily, she was pretty and well groomed, a tall woman with long, blonde hair and a radiant glow to her skin. But on this evening, her locks were lank, her skin pallid and she was terribly thin. My mum was only twenty-eight, but tonight she looked more than twice her age.

I returned to the lounge, where Gary was perched at the window, smirking at me and seemingly unconcerned at my mother's illness. Dad was still sitting where I had left him, Senior Service cigarette in one hand and a can of beer in the other. When he finished, the cigarette butt would join the many others which lay in a full ashtray and the tin would be thrown into an old cardboard box which rattled with empties. The beer cans were always there, a constant reminder of the fact that Dad drank all the time, yet he never seemed to be drunk. I couldn't understand this. When I watched television, men would drink beer and then reel around in drunkenness, often falling over, or singing, and having a great time. That wasn't my dad. That wasn't how drink affected him. I had concluded that my dad must not drink as much as those men, because, apart from sometimes falling asleep in his chair, I'd never seen him fall prey to the funny antics of the drunk men on telly.

In fact, my dad wasn't a funny man at all.

Tonight, as I came back from seeing Mum looking like death, from watching her retch her very insides out, I would realise just how bad his temper could be. His anger seemed to ooze out of him as he turned to me and barked, 'For fuck's sake, stop harassing your mother.' I was shocked – I couldn't remember Dad ever swearing at me before, even though he had never been particularly loving or warm. He was a man who believed in standards, he was Army through and through, but now he seemed to have forgotten that he was talking to a little girl.

I stood there staring at him, stunned by the bad words which had come out of his mouth.

'What are you fucking gawping at?' he snapped. 'You know she isn't well, you know she's ill, and Christ knows when she'll get any better.'

I'm not sure that I did know that. I did have an awareness that my mum was often sick, and that she was being sick more often these days, but at five years old I never thought about the future and I didn't put two and two together. Sometimes I felt sick if I ate too many sweeties, and I knew my friends did too. I certainly hadn't faced up to the possibility that there was something seriously wrong with Mum that might not get fixed.

My dad's words snapped me out of my reverie. 'Keep the

fuck away from her,' he told me. 'In fact, clear up your rubbish instead of standing there being useless. It's your bedtime, so hurry up for Christ's sake. Get all of your shite out of the way – move it!'

The unfairness of it swamped me. 'It's not rubbish, it's my homework!' I said, desperately wanting to cry. My mum was ill, my dad was swearing at me, my brother was calling me names, and my world seemed overwhelmingly horrible. I grabbed my homework jotter and books from where Gary was sitting, ignoring the fact that he was sniggering at Dad's treatment of me, and ran down the hallway to my bedroom.

I threw it all down onto my dressing table and flung myself on the bed. Just as I did so, I heard a horrendous crack and saw flashes of light. This was a ghastly night and it was getting worse. I hated thunderstorms and felt a knot in my stomach as the night got threateningly dark. I could hardly see anything. Despite an ominous feeling, I knew I had no alternative but to go back through to the lounge. 'Dad! Dad!' I screamed. 'I'm so scared. What's happening? When will it stop, Dad?'

He was as still as a statue as I stood beside his chair. I was a tiny child, terrified and desperate for some consolation. I couldn't go to my mum and my dad was acting in a way I simply couldn't comprehend. He wouldn't even look at me. 'Shut up. It's only a fucking storm. Now get your arse back into bed and stop being so bloody annoying.'

Tears were brimming in my eyes as I pleaded with him. 'Can I stay up for a little while, just until it stops? Please? Please, Dad?'

He finally turned round and looked at me. It chilled me to the bone. His face was alien and his eyes cold, almost as if he had no recognition of the child before him. Looking back, and knowing what was to come, I believe something had broken in my father that night. Given how my world was to shatter, beginning in only a few hours' time, it was as if he himself was unable to react to how he was behaving. The swearing, the aggression, the lack of eye contact – all these things were part of a personality which he may have used in his day-to-day life in the Army, but they were not part of the make-up of a loving father.

'If I have to tell you one more time, you little bastard . . .' he muttered menacingly.

He didn't.

I could feel the atmosphere. I could sense the tension.

As Mum writhed in agony in her own room, my own body felt a wave of fear. I was filled with the knowledge that this was a battle I couldn't win. As I scurried back to my room, the storm raged outside – and the one which would rip my life apart was only just beginning.

CHAPTER 2

FUN

As I lay in bed, I watched the storm. There was no point in trying to sleep; I was scared of the noise and of the flashes, scared of how Dad had treated me and of his words, which had made me realise how ill Mum was.

The blocks of flats surrounding where we lived were all alike during the day: grey, drab and peeling, desperately in need of some refurbishment. Ours was no different to the others, but the storm was changing things. The flats were washed in the glow of lightning, and the streaks of brilliant white sky were coming around more and more quickly. They changed from white to orange and then blue. My dressing-table mirror was reflecting all of this, and I was amazed by the kaleidoscope surrounding me. I wasn't a scaredy-cat. I was a big girl. A brave girl.

I snuggled down underneath the blankets. Perhaps other things would get better too. Perhaps, just as I had imagined the storm was a terrifying thing, I had imagined that Dad had been mean to me, that Mum would never get better again. Perhaps everything would be fine in the morning.

I'm glad I had that optimism – even if it didn't last.

I lay there, torn between fear and wonder at the light display which was flickering across my room. I clung to my golliwog, one of the few possessions I owned, and tried to sleep. I closed my eyes very tightly, but the flashing shards of colour from the storm still seemed to register. Eventually I fell into a fitful sleep.

I don't know how long it lasted, but sometime later that night, more likely the early hours of the morning, I was awoken by something – voices maybe, shouting or some other commotion. The storm had stopped, but there was something else brewing. There was a low droning noise, which, in my sleepiness, I finally identified as voices. As I listened, I could pick out those of my dad and also of Agnes Anderson, Mum's friend who lived in the same block as us. For a moment, I thought the storm had come back because there was still something playing out on the walls of the room. I rubbed my eyes and sat up, finally identifying it as a bright blue light shining upwards towards my window. But when I looked out, I saw something which made my stomach lurch – it wasn't lightning, it was an ambulance.

I ran out into the hallway and found the source of the noise which had woken me. There was a group of people there: two ambulancemen in green uniforms and Gary were standing beside my dad and Agnes. I wormed into the middle of the group easily, as I was so small, only to be grabbed by my father pulling at my nightdress. He stared down at me, his gaze unflinching, as I heard Agnes say, 'Let me take the kids for the night, Harry; you've got enough on your plate.' Dad dragged his eyes away from me to answer her. 'No. They're staying here.' He was scaring me by that point, just as he had before I'd fallen asleep. He was acting in a very calm, intense, controlled way and, as no one had yet told me what was happening to my mum, I felt panicked. Agnes noticed this and tried again. 'Well, at least let me take Tracy. She looks terrified, poor wee thing.' I knew instinctively that was what I wanted.

'Let me go with Agnes, please let me go with Agnes!' I begged. Somehow, I just knew that I needed to get away from my father, but he wouldn't budge. There was something so alarming about the look in his eyes – I didn't recognise it but knew I had to escape. He refused my pleas, rejected the offer from Agnes, and kept a firm grip of my wrist as Mum was carried out of her bedroom on a stretcher. I realised then that there was a doctor in the house too, and both he and the ambulancemen looked very serious.

Mum had been sedated and was oblivious to everything; and the fact that she was so still and so unlike my mummy started me crying. I wanted her to hold me. I wanted her to tell me that everything would be all right. I had a terrible feeling that if she didn't say those words, things would never be the same again.

I was right.

I was so right.

Dad told me and Gary to go into the lounge and, as we

did, I could hear Agnes try again. 'I'll just take Tracy,' she said breezily, as if my dad's previous rebuttals had never happened. 'I can make sure she gets to school tomorrow and then pick her up afterwards. She'll be fine with me, Harry. I'll keep her safe.'

Those words are imprinted on my mind. We don't remember everything about our childhoods, but there are some scenes we all keep locked in our memories as if they happened only yesterday. That one, the one of my mother being taken away on a stretcher and of Agnes trying to get me away, is burned in my memory. Did Agnes suspect something? Why was she so insistent? She was a good, kind woman, but I do wonder why she was so keen to get me in particular away from my dad, rather than Gary as well. What was she picking up on?

Whatever her thoughts, whatever she sensed, she failed. My father grabbed her firmly by the arm and escorted her to the open door. 'Leave now, Agnes. I've said "no". We don't need your help, we're fine on our own. Tracy is my daughter. I've made my decision.' He closed the door on Agnes without another word. For some reason, the moment he did that, a wave of dread came over me.

Dad came into the lounge, lit another cigarette and opened another can of beer. The room was filled with silence and he stared at me for a few minutes with no glimmer of emotion on his face. I wrapped my flimsy nightdress tightly around me and squirmed into the softness of the sofa. Gary was unusually quiet too, keeping his eyes down and saying nothing. Finally, the silence broke. 'Get yourselves back to bed. Now.' We both scuttled off the sofa and ran through to our rooms, where I fell asleep much more quickly than I expected, no doubt glad of the comfort and safety of my own bed after such an emotionally exhausting late night.

I woke up next morning to the sound of Dad swearing yet again. 'Up! Up! Fucking move it! Get your arse through for breakfast now.' I was confused when I got there to see an empty table. 'Where is it then, Dad?' I asked, sitting down. Standing behind me, he slapped the back of my head with such force that my forehead hit the wooden table. 'Your breakfast will be there when you fucking get it,' he snarled. 'Get something for your brother as well – and make me a cup of fucking tea.'

I was stunned and hurting. I was only little and was used to being told to keep away from the kettle and hot things, not being told to make cups of tea. I stood up, but was flustered – was Dad tricking me? Did he really want me to do this? His next words left me in no doubt. 'Move it, I fucking said! Or do you want another slap?'

I went to the cupboard, choking on my tears and rubbing my forehead. He had never hit me before. Just like his swearing, his violence was totally out of character; it was as if he was a new daddy, someone who had been brought in when my mum was ill the night before. He looked like my father, but his voice and his actions, his words and his behaviour, were totally foreign to me. I had to accept that I was at risk of being hit again if I didn't do what he wanted, even if what he wanted was so hard for me to grasp. He was making it very clear that no matter what he told me to do, I had to do it. Go to bed. Go to sleep. Keep away from Agnes. Stay with him. Make tea. All of it was at his command.

I dragged two stools to a place in front of the worktop and climbed up on my tiptoes to take breakfast bowls and cornflakes from the cupboard. I had watched Mum do this a hundred times, and although I had to stretch and make sure I didn't wobble or drop things, I knew I could do it. My little hands were shaking, but I pretended I was getting a teddy bear's picnic ready and focused on the job in hand. I reached down with everything, one thing at a time, while I stayed on the higher stool. I could feel my dad's eyes burning into the back of me as I climbed down and got the milk from the fridge. It splashed out of the bowls, over the top of the cornflakes I had poured, and I paused, wondering if he was going to hit me again, but nothing happened. I looked at him questioningly and he moved his eyes to the china mug in front of him, then flicked his gaze over to the kettle. I gulped and walked over, switching it on and realising that I had to do this.

Gary came in and asked what I was doing. One look at the red mark on my forehead and the tears on my cheeks silenced him. He hurriedly ate his breakfast as I struggled with the full kettle and, against all odds, managed to make my first ever cup of tea. It should have been a moment of triumph but it was far from that. I could feel sweat pouring down the back of my nightdress. So much was going wrong and Mum had only been away a few hours. I was in charge of feeding everyone and I was five years old. Was this going to continue until she came back? Was I now a grown-up? How many slaps would come with that role?

Thankfully, the drama of making breakfast and using the kettle had taken up a lot of time so, by the time it was all over, I had to get ready for school. Dad barked instructions at me again as I rushed through to my room and pulled on my clothes. I tried to brush my hair as best as I could and then walked through to the living room.

'Are you walking me to school today?' I asked him.

'No, I'm fucking not,' he shouted, slumping into his chair with a can of beer and cigarette already in his hand, despite it being eight o'clock in the morning.

Although I had been going to school on my own for a few days now, which was what I'd wanted, I felt the need for someone to look after me that day. I looked imploringly at Gary, willing to even take a few pinches from him so long as it came with a bit of brotherly care, but he sneered at me, muttered 'baby' and ran out of the door before I could even hoist my satchel onto my shoulders.

I wandered down the stairs and waited for Debbie and the others at our usual meeting place, saying nothing about what had happened as we walked along. The morning passed uneventfully and school finished at lunchtime, as it always did on Fridays. I had a childlike happiness at the prospect of freedom. I saw Gary playing football with his friends as I walked home and wondered whether he might be the one to get into trouble – we usually had to go straight home after school, and I could only think he was taking advantage of Mum not being there while forgetting how horrible Dad had been since yesterday. As I trotted along with my friends, I started to feel a little brighter. Perhaps Mum would be back? Maybe the doctors had made her all better and I could forget last night and this morning, as if it were all a nightmare.

When I got to the block of flats, I ran up the steps two at a time. Opening the front door, which was on the latch, I ran down the hallway. 'Mum! Mum!' I shouted, stopping in my tracks when I entered the lounge and saw only Dad sitting in his chair.

'She's not here,' he said, as he saw my eyes flicker around the room. 'They're keeping her in hospital – where's Gary?' I told him my brother was still playing football with his friends, expecting an explosion of anger, but instead Dad just nodded as if this was a good thing. 'That gives us time,' he reflected.

'Time for what?' I asked cautiously.

He paused at my question, as if wondering what to say next, then abruptly stood up and said, 'Come on, follow me.' He walked towards the bedroom he shared with Mum, then smiled at me. It wasn't how he had been for the last day or so, and I was confused again at how quickly his mood and character seemed to change. 'We'll change the bed,' he announced. 'Your mum was sick on the sheets. Go on. Strip the bed.'

I was bewildered – Dad was smiling but, yet again, he was asking me to do something I had never done before. He had offered me no help when I'd had to boil the kettle and make a cup of tea that morning, so why would he help me with this new challenge? The bed looked massive to me, and I didn't really know where to start. A sense of relief flooded through me when Dad seemed to read my thoughts. 'I'll show you how to do it. Don't worry. I'll tell your mum that you did it on your own and she'll be so proud of you that it will help her to feel better. You'd like that, wouldn't you?'

Of course I would! I gave Dad my biggest smile and started work, following his instructions.

'Pick up the quilt, Tracy,' he began, 'and undo the buttons at the bottom of it.'

This took quite a while. I was still mastering buttons on my own clothes, but they were easier to open than do up, so I managed eventually. Dad was sitting on a chair at the side of the bed, watching me and telling me what to do. 'Pull the cover off,' he continued, then he told me to take the pillowcases and bottom sheet off too. I was so pleased with myself. I was being a good girl for Mum and Dad while I did all of this hard work. 'Well done, Tracy,' he said, 'now here comes the fun part!'

'What's next, Dad?' I asked, out of breath with my exertions.

'Putting on the clean quilt cover – it's a lot harder than taking it off, but I'll help you.' He stood, telling me to stand in front of him, and shook the cover out. He put his arms around me and told me to grasp the two corners he was holding. 'I'll put the quilt in and you grab it once the cover is in place. This is fun, isn't it?' he said. He was still smiling, but the smile seemed forced – and it didn't feel like that much fun, because his arms were tight around my little body and I knew I had no choice about being there. He was pushing into me and it was something that didn't feel nice at all. I wanted to break free of him, I wanted to get away, but I was still very much aware of how quickly his moods were changing since Mum had gone into hospital and I didn't want to risk things taking a turn for the worse again.

As we struggled with the cover, I felt his body press hard into my back, harder than before. I held the corners just as I'd been told, but he didn't let go. 'I've got it, Dad,' I said. 'I've got it.'

Behind me, he said nothing, but he was pushing his body into me, harder and harder. I wasn't tall, and my head was at the level of his crotch as he shoved and shoved into me.

'Dad!' I almost whispered. 'Dad – I've got the cover, you can put the rest of the quilt in.' He didn't move his body from mine, but he did take his hands from my arms and allowed them to travel down my body slowly, finally resting on my waist. 'Dad?' I whispered again. 'Dad? What are you doing?' I honestly didn't know what was happening. What could I have made of it at that age? All I realised was that he was rubbing his hands around my waist, pressing in as hard as he could to my body, and breathing in a funny way as if he had run up the stairs too quickly and couldn't catch his breath. His head had dropped forward and I could feel a warmth on my neck; there were little gasps as he made a strange noise.

Fun

As soon as the strange noise had finished, Dad loosened his grip on me.

'There,' he said, turning me around to face him. 'I told you that would be fun.'

The duvet and cover lay discarded on the bedroom floor, forgotten. My father walked towards the door and, with a final glance back at me, concluded. 'That was fun.'

It wasn't a question.

It wasn't a laughter-filled remark.

It was a command.

I stood there, confused and upset, with only one thing certain in my mind – no matter what my dad wanted me to believe, whatever had just happened was not fun.

CHAPTER 3

BEING A GOOD GIRL

After it happened, I wasn't quite sure what to think. I was only a little girl, barely more than five years old – looking back with the awareness and understanding of an adult is completely different. At that age, all I knew was that my mummy was in hospital and my daddy had turned horrible, seemingly overnight.

I didn't really know anything about bodies or the birds and the bees, I didn't know anything about what grown-ups did with each other in private – but I did know that what my daddy had just done was horrible. I didn't want to complain; well, I didn't want a slap again and something told me that if I said a word, that's exactly what I would be getting.

To my relief, just as these thoughts were running through my mind and Dad was rearranging himself, I heard Gary open the front door. 'Remember,' said Dad, 'that was fun. You did well, Tracy, you did well.'

That was all he said. He had used me to pleasure himself, and he didn't even look ashamed. With his few words, he left the bedroom to speak to my brother. I heard him welcome Gary back – 'Nice time, son?' – as I stood there, looking at the bed. Remembering it now, the main feeling that I know I had was one of confusion. I was so young. After being ill for such a long time, Mum had been taken into hospital. Hospitals seemed scary places to me, where doctors put needles into you and there were lots of sick people. That's where my mummy was, and since she had gone there, my daddy had been acting like a stranger.

He'd shouted at me.

He'd said swear words to me.

He'd hit me.

And now – what had he done now? I wasn't sure I even had the appropriate words for what had just happened. I'd been told it was fun, I'd been told I was a good girl, but what was *fun* exactly? What had I done that was *good*?

I heard my dad laughing with Gary, sounding like his old self. Chatting about football. Being *normal*. I thought about how my mum made the bed, and tried to copy her, tried to finish off the job I had been asked to do in the first place. I did as well as I could under the circumstances and went back through to the lounge. Dad and Gary were in the middle of a conversation about Mum's hospitalisation, and my big brother was asking, 'Why can't we go too? Why do we have to wait until Sunday?' I was glad he had asked that as it was the very question preying on my mind, but I was too scared to bring it up after Dad's reaction to Agnes last night. It just seemed everything to do with the whole issue was going to put him in a bad mood.

Dad didn't have to answer Gary as there was a knock at the door. Almost as if thinking about her had brought her there, he opened it to reveal Agnes. 'How's Valerie?' she asked, without any preamble. Dad didn't invite her in; in fact, he narrowed the space between them by closing the door a little more. 'Not too good. She needs rest. She needs peace and quiet.' He stared at Agnes. 'She doesn't need visitors.' That answered Gary's question and my own unvoiced ones as well as putting Agnes firmly in her place.

By this time, both Gary and I were standing beside our dad. Agnes smiled warmly at us. 'How are you kids doing?' she asked us directly. Before we could answer, Dad snapped, 'They're fine, they know what's going on.' He went to close the door on her, but Agnes pushed it back slightly. 'My offer still stands, Harry. I'll take those kids any time. I'll take them all weekend.' My heart was in my mouth and I crossed my fingers behind my back. Maybe if Agnes took us, Dad would be happier. I wouldn't be getting things wrong all the time, and he wouldn't have to shout at me. Then, my old dad would be back, and when Mum got home from hospital, everything would be back to normal. Even as I stood there, beside the man who had taken the first steps on his horrific campaign to rob me of my childhood, I was wondering how much of it was my fault – and whether it was just a one-off, something I had misinterpreted and which could be forgotten ... if only he would say 'yes' to Agnes.

He made a strange noise, almost snorting at her offer. 'No. Absolutely not. We can manage.' I have often wondered why Agnes kept trying. My dad was being very blunt in his refusal, but she didn't give up. 'Today then. I'll take them today. Or what about little Tracy? I could just take her. Give her something to eat. Leave her till suppertime, I'll give her a bath and get her all settled. Why not, Harry?'

My dad's eyes flicked over me. 'I've got someone coming in, Agnes. I don't need you. We don't need you.' With that, he slammed the door in her face and made his way back to the lounge, followed by Gary. I stood there, something in my little heart realising that a chance had been taken away from me. Dad had said that someone was coming to look after us, and that gave me a glimmer of hope, but I wanted to go with Agnes. 'Dad,' I began, going into the lounge. 'When is the lady coming to look after us? Who is she?'

'What?' he barked. 'You must be even more stupid than I thought you were. I only said that to get the interfering old cow out of my face. We don't need her poking her nose in. When I'm gone, don't answer the door – and stay away from the windows, or you know what you'll get.'

He only looked at me when he said all of this, and Gary seemed oblivious to the instructions or the threat. 'Can I go out and play when you visit Mum later?' he asked.

'Course you can, son,' Dad quickly assured him, as the unfairness of it all hit me. I was the one being kept inside. I was the one who wasn't to answer the door. I was the one being imprisoned.

'And you,' he hissed, narrowing his eyes at me as if I was something nasty he'd trod in. 'Clean up. Shut up. And remember – be a good girl.'

This was a phrase which was already filling me with dread, and it would be one which would become his code for so many awful things I couldn't even imagine at that stage. Gary's voice cut into my thoughts. 'I'm starving – what are we having for dinner?'

'Tracy – you know how to use the grill?' Dad asked.

I shook my head quickly and looked at the floor, wishing it would swallow me up. 'No. No, I don't. Please don't make me do that, Dad. I can't.'

'Shut up. You'll do exactly what I tell you to do. You're the woman of the house now and you'll do everything, *everything*, that needs to be done. Understand?'

'But I'm not meant to touch the grill, Dad,' I whimpered. 'Mum says it's too dangerous.'

'Bloody useless! Doesn't your mother teach you anything? You're a lazy little bitch – now get in that fucking kitchen. I'll show you once, and you'll learn, because I won't fucking show you twice.' He punched me in the back to get me moving and pushed me towards the kitchen, where we soon ended up with some half-burned sausages. I got a few slaps along the way, but I was just grateful I didn't have to put my body in front of his while he cooked.

There was something about the scenario which made me really uncomfortable. Now, I know it was the words he used rather than the actions or the casual violence which was now punctuating all of his time with me. Swear words were littering everything he said, whereas previously he would never have cursed in front of me. He was calling me a 'little bitch' with increasing frequency. But, more than anything, it was his constant reiteration that I was the 'woman of the house' which made my skin prickle with fear.

I went back to the kitchen with the empty plates, trying to carry all three of them at one time. I hadn't had to be told that it was my 'job' or that I would get no help. I dragged a little stool over to the sink, climbed up and ran hot, soapy water into the basin just as I had seen Mum do on countless occasions. There had been a few times when she had let me climb up there and wash a few bits for fun, when she was in a good mood and feeling well, but it seemed very different now. I had cried a lot over the past couple of days and, although I felt upset, there were no tears now. I knew I had to get on with things, and that's a terrible realisation for a small child. I don't think I had an acceptance of the abuse at that stage, because I didn't quite know what was going on or even what had happened, but I did know there had been a change and that cooking, cleaning and being hit was now the norm for me.

I stood there, my arms up to the elbows in sudsy water, and sent out a little prayer for Mum. We had never been a fairy-tale family, and I had never been showered with affection, but the way we had been previously was a picnic compared to the hell I was now living in.

I think people are almost immune to abuse in some ways. Although we talk about it far more now than in my childhood (and that can only be a good thing), it is sometimes too easy to think it is all in the past, or it must have been OK because the victim is still standing. It always needs to be put into context. I was five years old. I had seen my mother taken to hospital under terrifying circumstances. My dad was lying to people, telling me to stay indoors and not answer the door to anyone, even good people like Agnes. He had pushed me, slapped me, punched me. He had shoved his body into mine, rubbed against me and made those strange noises while he did it. And all of these bad things were the things I had to accept if I was to be a good girl.

The dishes were finished, so I gingerly crept along the hall. I wanted to go to my own bed in my own room; hopefully sleep would come quickly and tomorrow might be better. I had only gone a few steps when I heard him shout, 'Tracy! Where do you think you're going? Get your lazy arse back in here.'

I did as I was told. I'm not sure if I would have been left alone in my room anyway given that it was next door to his (something he would always make sure was the case wherever we moved). 'Sit,' he barked, as if I were a dog.

I sat.

'Have you cleaned up?'

I nodded.

'Can't you talk?' he snapped. I could see Gary grin. He always liked it when I was in trouble; I guess it deflected attention from him and lessened the chance that he was going to get told off.

'Can I go to bed, Dad?' I asked.

'At this time of night? Something wrong with you? I'll have to think whether there's anything else you need to do first.'

His words chilled me, but I knew Gary hadn't a clue about what could be the real meaning. Dad's gaze wandered again. I didn't know how much he had been drinking, as it was always difficult to gauge, as it never seemed to affect him. I don't know how long we all sat there – it was a while. Gary eventually went through to his own room, the one furthest away from where I was left with Dad, and I sat, as motionless as possible, trying not to draw his eyes to me. I remembered that he was meant to be going to hospital to see Mum soon, and that visiting hours were almost starting. I couldn't wait for him to leave.

'Are you going to see Mum tonight, Dad?' I asked, quietly.

It was ages before he finally turned and looked at me. He put his empty can down on the floor beside all the others he had accumulated throughout the day so far. He placed his half-smoked cigarette in the ashtray beside the dozen or so other butts. He was going to be in a right state when he finally did go in to visit his wife.

'Yes, yes, I am. But I won't be long, don't you worry. You're a good girl, Tracy. You've done well today. I hope you'll keep on being a good girl for me – you will, won't you?'

I nodded, relieved at the thought of him being away for a couple of hours, but knowing just what he had done last time he said I was a good girl. I didn't want that again.

I didn't want to be a good girl if that's what it brought me.

I didn't want to be his sort of good girl.

29

CHAPTER 4

A SMALL WORLD

When Dad left for hospital, Gary went out to play with his friends. I would have preferred it if Gary had stayed, as I was still a bit scared when there was no one in the house – but I was quickly realising that there were worse things than being alone. I decided to clean and tidy some more, desperately hoping I could keep on Dad's good side. I emptied the box which held the beer cans and tipped the contents of the ashtray into a bin liner. The smell of the cans was horrible and the stale stink of the ashtray made me feel queasy. It took me ages to get everything looking nice.

I sat down, my stomach churning, and thought about how things were in my little life. There were many hundreds of Army families on that base in Germany. We lived in a flat at the bottom of the whole base. It was a close-knit community in many ways – and I have no doubt that, had it been known what my father did to me as a child, he would have been ripped apart. Sadly, his methods of keeping me quiet would be too effective, my silence pretty much guaranteed as a result of the web of lies and threats he would weave around me. That day, when we had such 'fun' changing the bed linen, was the start of his campaign of abuse, the start of my realisation that this man, who presented himself as a hero and great guy to everyone, was nothing more than a sick pervert who preyed on my innocence.

Army life is a strange combination of the 'real' world and something so distinct, so protected and separated from that same real life, it is hard to describe to anyone who has never been part of it. No matter where you are, no matter which country or region, you generally still have your own shops, your own school, your own insular life. At least you did when I was a child growing up in such a world. Even when you move from one base to another, there is a huge familiarity to the lifestyle and surroundings, even if the accents outside change or the temperature is the opposite of what you were used to in your last location.

We had moved to Rinteln when I was four. Before that, when we lived in Singapore, I was too little to remember a huge amount, so Germany was the scene of my first real childhood memories. We lived in a street which had three blocks of housing. In each of those blocks were three homes. Every single one had the same layout – if you were in a three-bedroomed Army house in one part of the base, you could rest assured every other three-bedroomed house across the whole place would be exactly the same. In fact, when we returned to Germany some years later for my father's third stint there, we lived in the house in the block directly next door to the one we stayed in when he first started to abuse me. They were so similar that, one night, coming back drunk from the Army bar, Dad went into our old house, let himself in the unlocked door, and slumped down in a drunken stupor on a chair – completely unaware that it wasn't his home! There was nothing different about it at all, and he hadn't noticed a thing.

As an adult, I've often wondered whether this lack of identity in something so personal as where you live was part of my dad's increasing problems with his own identity. He changed from day to day, from posting to posting, and yet he had chosen a life in which he was expected to be the same, to show no emotion, to not even have a home which reflected his own idiosyncrasies.

I know, from talking to my brother and Mum in later years, that he presented the move from Singapore to Germany as an exciting, positive one. 'You'll love it,' he told Gary. 'There are loads of kids your own age, youth clubs, swimming groups – there's everything.'

Gary's response was typical of him. Straightforward, blunt – but completely lacking in sense.

'Nazis,' he said.

'What?' asked my dad.

'Nazis. That's what there is. It's Germany. It'll be full of Nazis. I hate Nazis.'

My dad told him to stop being so stupid. 'It won't be full of Nazis. The war's over, you stupid boy. Anyway, how many Nazis do you think there'll be in a British Army camp?'

My brother was unrepentant. 'But I don't like them. I don't like Nazis.'

'You won't see any bloody Nazis – even if Germany's still stuffed to the gunnels with them, they'll be on the other side of the fence.'

That was the end of that argument. Dad managed to convince Gary and Mum that the move would be a good one and, from what I've heard, he certainly seemed excited about it. I was too little to really be part of the discussions, but I was excited about the prospect of a new house and new friends. In Singapore, we had lived in a high-rise block of flats and there was very little to do. I rarely got to play outside, and had no friends to speak of, so Germany would be a novelty for me.

When we got there we did meet lots of people, but Gary was better at making friends than I was. I was a reserved child, extremely quiet, and I wasn't the naturally bubbly sort of little girl who drew others to her. I was allowed out to play a few times – but that would soon stop.

Gary was allowed out to youth clubs and football practice, he played on the camp with his mates, and he always seemed to be having a good time. Dad was very laid-back with him, and allowed him to go his own way. At first, I thought it unfair that I was so restricted while Gary lived the life of Riley outside of school; only later did I realise that his absence from home was a deliberate strategy by Dad to ensure he had access to me whenever he wanted. When Mum was in hospital and Dad visited her, Gary would be allowed out to play with only one rule – he wasn't to come back in until Dad gave him permission.

One of the things I remember very clearly about living in the base was that every house had a big walk-in cellar. They were almost like cages when you walked into them. Most parents let the kids do the cellars up themselves with whatever decoration they liked, to make them into private dens. We were all very much aware of the music and fashion trends from back home, and the cellars were a reflection of British, not German life. Radios would blast out hits of the time, and there was a constant soundtrack of the Monkees and the Beatles. Songs like 'I'm A Believer' and 'All You Need Is Love' were always playing on camp, from radios in houses, and in the kids' dens. When Mum was at home, she had her favourites, which seemed more 'grown-up' than the bands who were the noise of my childhood. Engelbert Humperdinck would croon 'Release Me' and 'The Last Waltz' in the kitchen, and I would wonder why she liked such sad-sounding songs.

The cellars of many people I knew were like snugs. All of the old, unwanted furniture from their houses would get put down there, so there was a real hotchpotch of stuff in every one. There would be soft furnishings, lamps, record players, radios, books, comics, and a very warm feeling from such messy comfort in most places. I always loved going to friends' cellars. Every time an Army family moved, their belongings would be transported in what were called MFO boxes. MFO stood for Military Forwarding Office or Military Freight, and the MFO boxes were used for sending personal possessions overseas. They were big wooden crates, rather like tea chests, and these were usually kept in the cellars too. They were made of four sheets of plywood with bendy tin riveted joints and an interchangeable pair of lids and bases, all kept together with half-inch screws. People would write the address of their posting on the outside and it would turn up at their new accommodation – this was back in the days when the Army did it all, long before major removal companies were brought in.

Families knew they would always be moved somewhere else, so were ready to go at a moment's notice, and would often keep things in the MFO crates for a quick move. The children would push the crates together to make tables, places to lie down, obstacle courses to climb over – there were many uses for those things, and I think they were the most common component of every cellar or den in Germany.

Needless to say, we weren't allowed to take command of our den. At that stage, I didn't know many children who were in the same position, but Dad was absolutely adamant that we were not allowed into ours, and it was not our property. I never did find out why he was so hardline about this, but I knew I would get knocked about if I as much as set foot in the place. I believe it was just another way to control us, to emphasise that his word was the law, no matter what was happening in other families. I know he kept all his old Army stuff from all his years in the forces in the old MFO boxes, but that was it. Gary used to harp on about us being allowed down there, but there was no room for manoeuvre. He just didn't want us to interact with other children – well, he particularly didn't want *me* to interact with other children. I was kept on a tight leash.

It was a very small world. News from back home would filter through, and British programmes on TV and radio were the norm, as we never really immersed ourselves in German culture, but we were also removed from things. The world was changing – huge new towns were being built in the UK which would change the landscape of the whole country, politicians were trying to gain access to the EEC, the National Front was emerging, and Britain's nuclear programme was growing stronger. None of it meant anything to a little girl in a different country, whose mum had been taken away and whose dad had turned into a stranger.

I had hoped for a happy life when we moved to Rinteln but, sitting there alone, such happiness seemed a world away. I heard a key in the lock of the door and sat up in the chair as my dad came in – despite being worried about him coming home, I desperately wanted to know how Mum was. He had six cans of beer in a plastic bag and threw them down on the floor next to 'his' chair. That explained at least part of how he intended to fill his evening – I could only hope it would be all. He looked around the room and I waited for what I hoped would be words of encouragement and some news of Mum. There was nothing. He sat down in his chair and kept looking at me.

'Come here,' he snapped.

I hesitated. 'How's Mum? Is she coming home soon?'

'She's fine,' he replied, but didn't answer my query about when she'd be back. 'Come here.'

I didn't move.

'I've told you twice, and I won't tell you again – come here.'

I may only have been five years old, but I knew he wasn't asking me to come to him for comfort. There would be no hugs from my dad, no reassurance that he would look after me while Mum was away, or that he would make it all better. How can a child that age possibly balance the two horrible options she is faced with? If I didn't go to him, he'd hit me, of that there was no doubt. The slaps and punches were getting more frequent, stronger. If I did go to him – what? What would happen? I was so young, so innocent, I didn't even have the words for what might occur. I couldn't actually conceive what he might be planning, but I sensed it would be awful, probably a damn sight worse than getting battered again.

As I took a few tentative steps towards him, I felt as if the walls were closing in around me. Just as I was inches away, his eyes boring into me, his gaze never flickering, I heard the door bang open yet again.

Gary flew into the room at the same time as our father jumped out of his chair. 'What the hell are you doing back?' he screamed.

'What?' stuttered Gary. 'I thought I was to come back when you got home from hospital. I thought you wanted me in.'

Dad pushed him back onto the sofa and jabbed him in the chest.

'You listen to me, boy, and you listen good. This is my house, and what I say is law. You go out when I tell you, you come back when I tell you. And you never – you *never fucking again* – come back inside this house until I tell you.'

He didn't have to say anything else. The look on Gary's face said it all. That was the only time Dad treated him the way he had been treating me, and Gary wanted no part of it. From that moment on, he would do as he was told – he would be a good son but a terrible brother, and he would close his eyes to everything that would happen.

As Dad had made so very clear, his word was law . . . and I would gradually find out just how far he would go to make sure I obeyed.

CHAPTER 5

EVERYTHING CHANGES

My world had changed so much since Mum had gone into hospital on the Thursday. She had been ill for a while, and I was almost used to the constant sickness and her saying she was unwell, but the fact that she wasn't physically there was new. For a five-year-old to see her mum being taken away like that, to be given very little information over what was happening and when (or if) she might come home again, was bad enough. But I also had to face up to Dad changing overnight, swearing at me, making me do things around the house that I knew a little girl shouldn't do, and then all the strange things which had occurred when I was told to change the bed. On top of it all, there was just a feeling, a change in the atmosphere that I couldn't put my finger on. I only knew it felt threatening – it felt bad.

The whole of Saturday was difficult – Gary had been allowed out to play with his friends, but I'd been kept at home again. Agnes hadn't called, so I didn't even have the possibility of an escape route. Both Gary and I knew by this time not to ask about Mum. We'd both get shouted at, there would be no information forthcoming, and I'd get a clip round the ear for my trouble. Initially, when Gary was out, I felt as if I was walking on eggshells. Dad kept me cleaning and tidying all day and, on the few occasions when I did sit down, I'd catch him staring at me. When I'd asked for breakfast, he'd hit me and asked why I couldn't make it myself. When I'd tried, he came and told me to make some for him and Gary too. I'd been hit again when I messed that up.

I was dreading him asking me to change the bed again – even though I had only done it two days earlier, there was something inside me thinking it could be used as a command again. As the day wore on, with Gary only coming back now and again for meals and snacks, I relaxed a little. There was nothing left to clean and I was allowed to sit by the table at the window, drawing and colouring. I tried to make dinner – potatoes and sausages – and was surprised when Dad didn't shout at me. Even I knew I'd made a bad job of it – the potatoes were undercooked, the sausages were burned, and everything was cold before it reached the table (and there were no microwaves in those days to rescue such meals).

At about 6pm, he told us to get ready for bed. It was early even for a five-year-old, given that it was the weekend. Gary complained a little, but didn't push things.

I trotted through to my bedroom and put my pyjamas on, before brushing my dark hair and cleaning my teeth. After I had gone through my usual routine, I went back to the living room where Gary was already sitting with Dad, watching television. As soon as I walked in, Dad stared at me. 'What the fuck are you wearing?' he snapped. I was confused – he'd told me to get ready for bed, and I had. What could I possibly have done wrong now?

'My pyjamas,' I stuttered. 'You told me to get changed.'

'I told you to get ready for bed – and that means put your nightdress on,' he bawled at me.

I felt hot, angry tears falling down my cheeks as I ran back to my room. Could I get nothing right? Was he going to shout at me for every little thing?

I struggled out of my pyjamas and into my winceyette nightie. It was getting too short for me and I had chosen my pyjamas as I wanted to be cosy, but I didn't dare defy Dad. I took a deep breath and went back through to him again. He nodded when I walked in this time. 'Better,' was all he said.

I sat beside Gary on the sofa, hoping we'd get to stay up a little longer. I was exhausted from cleaning all day, but there was something inside me saying that, if I was close to my big brother, even if there was no love lost between us, I'd be safe.

No sooner had I sat down than Dad spoke. 'Are you fucking deaf?' he asked. 'I told you to get ready for bed, and that means you're going to your fucking bed.'

Gary groaned but got up. I followed him.

'No,' said Dad, with menace in his voice. 'Him. Not you.'

'What?' Gary shouted, all thoughts of keeping Dad sweet disappearing with this unfairness.

'I don't mind going to bed, Dad,' I said. 'I want to. I'm really tired.'

He stared at me in a manner that I was becoming used to.

'Please,' I whispered. 'Please.'

'Gary, go. You,' he said, pointing at me, 'sit.'

My stomach was immediately in knots. What was I going to get in trouble for this time? I sat back down on the brown fabric sofa, trying to hide the fact that I was shaking, and pressed myself back into the cushions.

'Not there. Sit here. Beside me.'

I couldn't quite work out what he was telling me to do. He was sitting in what was known as 'his' chair. It was a sludgy olive-green fabric on a wooden frame and no one else was allowed to sit there. On top of that, there was only room for him.

'Where?' I asked.

'Here. Beside me,' he replied, patting the small bit of seat that was free beside him. He had squeezed over to the side of the seat, but there was very little spare space.

'I'm fine here, Dad,' I whispered. 'Shall I just go to bed?'

'No,' he hissed, 'you'll get your arse over here just like I told you to, you cheeky little bitch.'

I shuffled off the sofa, grudgingly, and wriggled myself into the chair beside him.

'Now,' he said, 'that's better, isn't it? That's nice. You think that's nice too, Tracy.'

He wasn't asking, he was telling me. He didn't look like he believed it either.

I had no idea what to say or do. Was I supposed to cuddle

him? Was I supposed to say I'd had enough of sitting beside him and ask to go to my room again? If he thought this was nice, then maybe I could bring up the one topic that was on my mind. I decided it was worth the risk.

'Dad?' I began hesitatingly, 'is Mum any better, is she coming home soon?'

He had been moving about beside me, as if he was trying to get comfortable, but he stopped when I spoke those words.

'Is that all you can think about? Is that all that you can say? Your mother, your mother, your mother?'

He paused.

'You know what, Tracy? It's time that you knew something. Your mother wants you to be a good girl. I want you to be a good girl. And do you know what good girls do? They listen to their daddies. They do as they're told. They make their daddies happy. And when their daddies think of nice things for them to do together, good girls are pleased about that – they don't keep fucking moaning when they should shut the fuck up.'

I tried to blink away the tears which were threatening to come again.

'Do you understand, Tracy? Do you actually listen to a word I say?'

'Yes, yes, I do, Dad. I'll try to be good, I really will,' I whispered. The thing was, I didn't know *how* to be good. All the things I thought made a good child had not been enough. I'd been trying already. I'd cleaned and tidied and cooked. I'd stayed at home, I'd kept quiet, and yet he was still acting as if I was very naughty.

'Do you want to know something else, Tracy?' he asked. 'There are lots of ways little girls can be good, and then ... there are some very special little girls who can be *extra* good.' His voice was softer now, and he wasn't swearing at me.

But he was doing something else.

As he spoke to me, alone in that room, his fingers, his rough horrible fingers, were pushing up the hem of my nightdress. At first I thought he was trying to pull my nightie down, to make sure it covered me. Actually, he was doing the complete opposite and it was an invasion of me from the moment he began.

The space between us on the chair seemed like nothing – there had been very little to begin with, but now his presence seemed overwhelming. He was pushing against me, just as he had done when we were changing the bedclothes, but this time I could see his face. It was contorted, it seemed as if he was in pain, but if he was, why didn't he stop? I couldn't work out why he was doing this, or why it was making him act this way. I knew nothing of sex. I had never walked in on my parents doing anything, I was too young to have giggly conversations with my friends. This was the 1960s, and there were no programmes on TV which may have made me older than my years, no constant background of soap operas, no music videos teaching me things before I should know them.

I was completely innocent – and completely at his mercy.

I simply couldn't work out what was going on. He was panting a lot, as if he had been running up the stairs.

What was that for? I wondered. He was only sitting in his chair, and yet he was getting so out of breath. He was sweaty and his hands were rubbing at my legs. They went up and down, up and down, his fingers wandering a little higher every time. I was scared that, if he wasn't careful, he would touch my private parts. A thought flashed through me of how awful that would be – and that I would probably get into trouble, even though he was the one doing it all. My thinking was so confused, because I had absolutely no frame of reference for what was being done to me.

He had pushed my nightie up so far by now, and I knew he would be able to see my bottom if I wasn't careful. I squirmed around on the chair and tried to work the fabric back down over me, but his hands were stronger. I couldn't understand this either. Why would he want to do this?

'Dad . . .' I started to say, but he told me to shut up before I could go any further. As he held my nightdress up with one hand, I could hear him panting more. His other hand went to his own trousers and he unzipped them, slipping his fingers inside and moving them around so quickly that it seemed to make him even more out of breath.

As he was doing this, he was saying words I knew were bad. He'd been calling me a little bitch all day, but now he was saying that I was dirty too. I wasn't. I really wasn't. I'd been cleaning all day and I'd always washed my hands, so why was he saying this? As he got more and more out of breath, his hand kept my nightdress pushed up over my front bottom and my back bottom. His words were getting faster and faster and he seemed to want to just tell me I was a *dirty little bitch* over and over again. He said it quicker and quicker, his voice got deeper and deeper, then, suddenly, he let out a moaning sound and flopped back, letting my nightie fall down.

He let out a huge breath and lay there with his eyes closed. What was I meant to do now, I wondered?

'Dad?' I whimpered, completely confused by what had just happened. 'Dad? Are you OK?' I didn't know if he was ill or sick; I already had one parent in hospital and now the only one I had left was in such a strange state that I wondered if the doctors would soon be coming for him too.

He opened his eyes and looked at me as if he hated what he saw.

'Get up,' he snarled, pushing me off the chair.

I hurried away from him, pulling my nightdress down as far as it would go as I headed towards the door.

'Where the fuck are you going?' he asked.

'To bed,' I replied, confused again. It seemed as if every time I did what he said, I got it wrong.

'No, you're fucking not. Dirty little bitch like you needs to get a wash. Now get to that bathroom and run a bath. Get in it and wait – don't close the door, don't lock the fucking door. You're filthy, absolutely fucking filthy. Get in there and wait for me.'

I did as I was told.

I did as I was told that time and the many, many times which were to follow. I had no way of knowing what was happening, that my father was laying down the ritual he would stick to for so many years. Looking back, I'm glad I didn't know. Glad I didn't know the horrors which were to come.

CHAPTER 6

RESPONSIBILITIES

We were allowed to go and visit Mum in hospital the next day. On the way up the stairs to the ward, Dad waited until Gary was ahead of us and pulled me back slightly. 'Remember what I told you,' he hissed. 'Your mum wants you to be a good girl – but she doesn't want you bothering her with all sorts of nonsense. If you want her to get home, you keep being good for me, and you speak only when you're spoken to.'

Mum looked slightly better, but the doctors still had no idea what was wrong with her. She said she hoped to be back home that week, but our visit was a short one. Gary spoke about football, while Dad walked around the room a lot and kept his eye on me – I sat quietly in a chair, terrified to say anything. There was no tearful reunion – we weren't that sort of family – and I heard no words of affection between my parents. I would have thought Dad would have paid more attention to his wife, told her he was missing her, but there was nothing like that. He didn't hug or kiss her, and we left within half an hour.

'Good, you did well,' he said to me, quietly, as we walked to the bus stop to get home. Gary was running ahead, kicking a can along the street, and couldn't hear him. When we got home, Dad made dinner. Maybe I was doing things right? However, every time I thought of the night before, I felt ashamed and sick.

What had happened on the Saturday night was awful. When I had run the water for my bath, Dad came into the bathroom after me. I thought he would be checking to see if the water was fine, as that's what Mum always did, even though she was the one who always got it ready in the first place. He didn't do that. Once the bath was full, he put the lid of the toilet seat down and parked himself on it.

I waited.

I didn't want to take my nightie off in front of him. Even at five I was too old for that, and I certainly felt uncomfortable about it given what had just happened.

'Get in,' he snapped.

'Are you going away?' I asked.

'Get in,' he repeated, ignoring my question.

I was so ashamed as I slid out of my nightie. Ashamed that he could see me. If he had been a normal daddy, it would have been fine. He would have checked the water, helped me in, kept the door open a little to make sure I was safe; but none of this was normal, none of it felt like it was to look after me. It felt as though it was all about what he wanted and needed. As I washed myself, he stared at me, and I felt his eyes burn into me as he leaned closer. He kept looking at the door, as if to confirm to himself that it was closed – to this day, I always keep the bathroom door ajar when I'm having a soak.

I tried to get out after a few minutes, but he poked my shoulder with his finger. 'You're going nowhere,' he said, 'dirty little girls need to make sure they're properly clean.'

'I am, Dad,' I said, 'I am.'

He snorted. 'I'll be the judge of that. Wash.'

I started all over again. There wasn't much of me to wash in the first place, but I went over every part of me with the flannel and soap just to make sure.

'Harder,' he told me.

I did as I was instructed until he finally spoke. 'Out. Move yourself.'

I clambered over the rim of the bath with no help, and tried to dry myself as best I could. Again, he offered no assistance and didn't try to touch me – he just stared and stared and stared. What I didn't know was that this would prove to be one of his requirements almost every time he abused me. His need for me to have a bath, and his need to watch me while I was in there, would be a major component of what he did to me. He would never touch me while I was in there, but he would always stare nonstop in a way I couldn't comprehend. Was he trying to work out what had happened, what he had just done to me? Was he trying to make me feel worse, as if I had not a shred of privacy, nowhere at all to hide from him? I don't know. I'll never know.

When I was dressed again – in clean pyjamas, not the nightie which represented the shameful things he had done – he walked out of the room without a word and I quietly went to my bed, where I was left alone.

Over the next few days, my life acquired a pattern of sorts. I'd go to school as normal, but I wasn't allowed to have contact with anyone outside of that time. I couldn't have friends round, I couldn't go to visit anyone else. I had to cook and clean, I had to tidy and organise. As my dad had told me, I was the woman of the house. He never spoke of what had happened, and I didn't dare bring it up. I had no conception really of what had gone on anyway – I didn't have the words for it or the awareness of how wrong it had been. All I knew was that I didn't like it, that he was in charge, and that I never wanted it to happen again.

After a week, Mum came back home – there were no fanfares, no celebrations, she was just there one day when I got back from school. If she'd missed me, she didn't say. If she had any suspicions over what had gone on, I wasn't aware of them. What I did know was that it didn't last. The sickness started up again and the sores all over her body started appearing. It would be the start of years of hospitalisations. I suppose I had been aware of her symptoms starting up again but at the same time I didn't want to consider the possibility that she might go away as she had before. When I left for school in the mornings, she was often up being sick already. When I came back, she had a horrible grey pallor to her and I knew she was in pain. She didn't always try to hide it and I would hear her groaning in agony. I had no idea what was wrong – which was unsurprising, given that the doctors were all perplexed too.

One day, a few weeks after the night which had started it all, I got home from school and Mum had gone. I rushed in the door and realised there was no sound of her vomiting. Dad was sitting in his chair, in his Army uniform, a can of beer in his hand, smoking as he always did.

'Where's Mum?' I asked, although I knew the answer. I could sense her absence, if that makes sense; it felt different from when she was at the bingo or had just popped out to the shops.

He always took his time to answer me, unless he was shouting or telling me I was in trouble straight away. It seemed like an age passed before he told me the inevitable truth.

'Hospital.'

There was no sugar coating or comfort.

'Come here,' he demanded.

'Why?' I asked.

Another pause.

'What sort of fucking answer is that? I'm your father, I said "Come here" so you should fucking jump.'

I stood still.

'How stupid are you? Come here.'

I moved forward a few steps. He was in his khaki trousers and shirt, all the usual gear. Even at home, I seldom saw him in civvies. He seemed to need that uniform, need the status it brought him even in his own house. His eyes were dark, hard, unfeeling. All I wanted was a daddy who would take me in his arms, in all innocence, and hug me as he told me that my mum would be better soon. I wanted him to tell me that he loved me, to make up for the loss of my mum and be the dad he should be, not the monster he had shown himself capable of becoming.

'Do you know why your mum is back in hospital?' he asked me. I shook my head. 'It's because of you. It's all your fault, Tracy.'

Just as he said those horrible words, the door slammed and Gary came in.

'Where's Mum?' he asked, just as I had done.

Dad's response was always warmer towards him, and he didn't swear at Gary nearly as much as he did at me. 'She's in hospital, son. Now, go through to your room, get changed and get your homework done.' Gary did as he was told, leaving me alone with Dad again. 'Now, where was I?' he pondered, falsely. He knew exactly what he had been saying to me. 'Ah, yes. Your mum. In hospital again. Thanks to you, Tracy, all thanks to you.'

'I didn't do anything, Dad, honestly I didn't.' Even to my own ears, my voice sounded pathetic.

'Are you sure?' he asked.

'I've been a good girl.'

'No. No you haven't. And do you know how I know that? It's because, if you'd been a good girl, your mum wouldn't have had to go back into hospital.'

Just as he said this, Gary came back through with his school bag and sat down at the table.

'What are you doing?' asked my dad.

'Er, homework,' Gary stated obviously.

'Not in here you're not.'

53

'But you told me to do it,' he responded, much more bravely than I ever would have done.

'I told you to go to your room and do your homework. And that's where you'll go,' he said, as Gary sighed dramatically and picked up his things. 'Take these with you,' he added, throwing his Army boots at my brother. 'Get the polish and bull the buggers until I can see my face in them. I'll come through and check on you when I decide. You stay there. You understand?'

Gary nodded, sighed some more and left the room. This, I would soon discover, would be one of my father's strategies. When he wanted Gary to be distracted and focused on some petty task that he had to get right for fear of incurring my dad's wrath, he'd get sent to his room, usually to bull the boots. This meant the boots had to be rubbed with polish or beeswax until they were as shiny as possible, and Dad always liked to get a bit of glory for how well they had been done – from this point on, I don't ever remember him doing them himself, he always got one of us to do it for him, usually as a punishment for me or a distraction for Gary.

He turned his attention back to me once Gary had closed the living-room door behind him.

'Come here, Tracy,' he said, quietly. I walked towards him, my heart heavy with the knowledge that whatever was going to happen was inevitable. I couldn't get out of anything my dad decided to do to me, and there was no one there to save me. 'What is really important is that you understand what is going on.'

I could feel myself wanting to argue with everything he said. *I understood nothing.*

'You're a big girl now.'

No, I'm not, I wanted to say. *I'm little, I'm only five, and I want you and Mum to look after me.*

'You need to start realising that you have responsibilities and that when bad things happen, it's your fault.'

I don't want responsibilities, I want Mum to be OK, and I want you to stop hitting me and doing those horrible things to me.

'Listen to me, Tracy – this is really important.'

I held my breath as he pulled me towards him.

His hands travelled up my body and he wrapped his legs around the side of me.

'Your mum is ill because of you.'

No! That can't be right, I thought, *I haven't done anything to Mum.*

'But you can make her better too. Do you understand, Tracy? When you're a good girl, it makes Mum better. When you don't do the ... things that make you a good girl, Mum ends up in hospital. She got home, didn't she?' I nodded. I couldn't argue with that. 'She got home because you had been a good girl, but then you started being bad again. And now she's back in hospital and only you can sort that out. You need to be good. You have to be good.'

I may have only been small, and I may have previously worried that I wouldn't understand, but I understood all too clearly now. The only times he had told me to be a good girl was when he had done nasty things to me, when he pushed himself on me, and rubbed himself on me, and touched me. When he panted and breathed strangely, when he watched me in the bath and he called me a dirty little bitch.

When all of that happened, and when I let it happen, I was a good girl.

When I was a good girl, Mum got better.

'It's easy really, Tracy,' he whispered, his hot, smelly beer breath in my ear. 'You need to be a good girl. There are things to do that will make you a good girl. It's really important to remember that good girls keep . . . the secret, because, if you tell, Mum will get ill. She'll become more ill than she's ever been before and it will be all your fault. I'm sure you don't want to be the one who puts your mum into hospital, do you, Tracy?' I shook my head as he spoke. 'But you will – you will if you don't keep the secret and do what you need to do. There's nothing wrong with it, you just shouldn't bother your mum. It's up to you, it's all up to you.'

Everything was falling into place. If I wanted Mum home, I had to do those things, I had to let him do those things. I had done them and she had come home; when I didn't do them, when he didn't try to make me do them, she had got ill again.

As he told me all of this, the tears rolled down my cheeks. I felt his hands all over me, his fingers in places they shouldn't have been, as he said over and over again, *good girl, dirty little bitch, good girl, dirty little bitch . . .*

All I could think was, *I'm doing it for Mum, this will make her better, I'm doing it for her.*

CHAPTER 7

THE LOVING COUPLE

Dad was his usual self outside of the family home – a great guy, admired by all – while at home, every time Mum was in hospital, he was abusing me. Over the next six months, she was hospitalised a lot, but the nature of her illness, which was still undiagnosed, meant she was also perfectly well at times. On those occasions, she seemed to like to spend as little time as possible at home. She loved bingo, and went there as often as she could, and she loved spending time with friends and neighbours. They weren't a loving couple and didn't seem to need to spend time together. In the past, Dad had made comments about her going out, especially about her 'wasting' money at the bingo, but now he seemed to positively encourage it. It doesn't take a lot to work out why – an empty house was all he needed.

When people ask me what my dad looked like, I find it hard to describe him in some ways – there was nothing remarkable about him at all. People tend not to have 'evil' tattooed on their foreheads. I feel that what he did to me should have made him noticeable in some ways. People didn't seem to see anything was the matter with me, no matter how I tried to make them as the years went on; but surely, I often thought, surely others would sense a monster in their midst. They didn't.

The truth is, Dad was amazingly unremarkable. He was quite short, and had a medium build which would turn towards fat later on in his life. Despite the fact that he loved to brag about being in the Army, he was only a clerk. He got the uniform, he got the kudos, but he wasn't off saving lives or risking his own. He spent all day every day sitting on his backside, so, unless he was away on a six-week exercise, he would have no activity at all – unless constantly lifting cans of beer to his mouth counted. I never saw him do an assault course, I never saw him run, but he wasn't a clerk because he had injuries or a disability, he had simply chosen that role. He always said he chose it so he could have a trade, but he didn't actually have one of those either as far as I could see.

As I got older, I realised he was the living embodiment of someone who had his cake and ate it – he was in the Army, but not in the Army. He had the respect and glory, but he did bugger all to acquire it. I've known brave men, I've listened as their deaths have been reported, and I can assure you my dad did not possess one ounce of courage in his character. It used to hurt me so much when he told people he was in the armed forces, that he had been based in Northern Ireland during the Troubles for a while, and they would respond with respect. Without going into detail, he never had to say how little he did, he just had to say the magic word 'Army' and people thought he was a hero. He was a disgrace to all those brave men and women who do justice to their position.

My dad was in it for the role he played. He loved his uniform. He loved how people looked at him when he walked by in it, and he took enormous pride in that symbol of his status. He adored being on parade and he needed everything to be immaculate. But, of course, I did the bulk of the work to make things that way. I was the woman of the house, after all. I made everything shine, I made everything glisten, and he just stood there – a big man in a safe job.

That was definitely his persona and, while there are many good, decent men in the Army, there are also far too many like him, cheery with everyone else, but staunch disciplinarians within the home, making their wives' and kids' lives a misery. They love having a sense of authority and yet they're often not the ones actually doing anything in the front line. That was him. He had a light moustache, jet-black hair, dark eyes, a real Mediterranean look. He always had his hair short and Brylcreemed. He smelled of Old Spice aftershave and stale cigarettes, and I still feel sick when I get a whiff of him from another man.

My mum was almost the same height as him, maybe an inch shorter, and she had a very distinctive mole on her cheek. She was slim and good-looking, with long, thick white-blonde hair which she wore in a beehive. That beehive was her pride and joy, and she must have kept the hairspray industry in business for years! I remember one night when we had only just arrived in Rinteln, I woke up in the early hours to the sound of her screaming. I rushed through to their bedroom, which held no horrors for me at that time, to find my dad swatting at her head as she continued to shriek the place down. We'd spent the whole day unpacking MFO boxes until late, and she'd fallen asleep with her clothes still on only to be woken by dozens of cockroaches crawling all over her. They'd come from the boxes and seemed to have set up camp in her beehive! It was one of the few funny moments I can remember in my childhood, although any humour was soon dismissed the next day when she had to go and get it all hacked off.

It soon grew back and returned to being her crowning glory. Mum was a handsome woman with very high cheekbones which she never complemented with make-up. Her face was always scrubbed clean and her clothes in particular. It was the 1960s and most women were wearing short skirts – my mum was no exception and she had a preference for tight-waisted dresses which were halfway up her thighs. She never wore trousers and always took good care of herself when she could.

While my dad liked to smell of Old Spice, Mum's perfume of choice was Tweed. She liked to be surrounded by smelly stuff and always bought Avon products. Wherever we lived, there was an Avon rep on camp, and Valerie was a good customer. She especially liked their soaps, which came wrapped in tissue paper inside pretty little boxes, often with a drawer you would slide out. I remember soaps in the shape of bells, umbrellas, and flowers aplenty. We had pelmets and mantelpieces covered in them and Mum placed them all around the house.

The women on camp would hold Avon or Tupperware parties where they all congregated in a house. They'd take turns every six weeks or so, and there would be about eight of them at each one. Mum tended to go with Agnes to these and they'd all take turns at providing sandwiches, tea and cake if they were the host. The parties would be held in the early evening and kids would play outside together until they were finished two hours later. They gave the women an opportunity to catch up on any news and gossip. Mum tried to host one once but Dad was horrified when he came home early and caught her; she was told never to hold one again. After this, she went to the other women's houses, refusing to take me and Gary. Her excuse was that the women wouldn't want us two eating their sandwiches when they couldn't bring their kids to our house. I remember feeling it was another form of alienating me from 'normal' life. I had to stay home when she went to one, whereas Gary would do his own thing and wait for Mum outside the house and come home with her later.

She enjoyed being with friends, who she would pick up quite easily wherever we moved – they were never hugely close, but Army wives have to learn to be quick at making new female friendships, and they can't get too tied to each other either.

When I list the things my mum liked, to me, it seems

quite a lot. Perfume and Avon, soaps and bingo, friends and fashion.

But she never liked me.

I know that lots of children, at whatever stage of their life, may make that claim. Their mum doesn't understand them, or she's too strict, or she's too bossy, or a million other things. However, I can categorically say, with hand on heart, that my mother simply didn't like me.

I only have one photograph of us together. We're on holiday in Clacton and she has her bouffant hair standing firm against the sea air. I'm grinning like a Cheshire cat and she's completely blank-faced. There isn't a glimmer of emotion and, to be honest, the camera isn't lying. That's how I remember her – she was never warm towards me, never tactile, never loving. I felt as if I was a nuisance, as if I was just someone who got in between her and Gary because, my God, she was the opposite with him. She loved her boy. When she came back from hospital, he was the one she looked for. She would hug him and say how glad she was to be home, and all the time she would be looking at Gary and blanking me.

As a grown woman, I tried to work out what the relationship between my mum and dad truly was in the hope that it could throw some light on what my life was like, but the pieces I do have don't make enough sense. I never saw him hit her, although he was handy enough with me, but she did once tell me that when she was pregnant with me, they had a huge argument about something. Dad grabbed her on the arm and left a thumbprint which lasted for the rest of her pregnancy. The odd thing is that I have a birth-mark on my arm in exactly the same place – in the shape of a thumbprint. Perhaps he was even making his mark on me in the womb.

Theirs was not a passionate relationship. They didn't even seem to be good friends. They were very distant with each other and had quite a traditional relationship – Mum's role was to stay at home, cook, clean, and look after the children. These were pretty much the same responsibilities Dad handed over to me when she was in hospital – plus the ones in the bedroom. I never saw him buy her flowers, or kiss her, or hold her hand. When he visited her in hospital, he never took anything as a gift or gesture. He would sit on the end of the bed as if he couldn't wait to get away and there was no feeling to any of their interaction together. He was completely cold-hearted, with never a lingering look behind him as he left, or a sign that he was worried about the mother of his children.

As a wife and mum myself, I know children do not always see the reality of their parents' relationship. In a bad marriage, adults can hide things from their kids to spare them hurt, but in a good one, children often just don't pick up on little in-jokes, or warmth which has come from a life's journey together. I couldn't see a single thing which kept Mum and Dad together in all the years they were married. I never caught them having a sneaky cuddle or kiss, he never playfully pinched her or tickled her when he thought we weren't looking. I never caught them laughing about something we weren't privy to. We all know that passion can die with any couple, but there is usually something left – I saw nothing with them. Even when Mum was at death's door, when you would expect a husband to show some kindness, be at a loss, it just gave him an excuse to be with me.

Of course, I don't know the whole story. I do know she wasn't close to her family back home either, so perhaps there was just something in her nature that made her unable to form relationships (although that wouldn't explain why Dad was the same, or why she was loving to Gary). In fact, back where they came from in Scotland, no one seemed to have any time for her. One time, when she was in hospital, Dad took us to Scotland as he said my granny would need to look after us as he was busy (I don't know what he was doing, as he usually took every opportunity to be alone with me). When we turned up at her house, I realised it was completely unannounced and my gran – a complete stranger to me – had no idea we'd planned to arrive. She opened the door, took one look at us standing there with our bags and said, 'They're not coming here – they belong to that bitch.' My dad said nothing, just dragged us back to the bus stop and took us to his sister. I never saw my granny again and never did get any explanation, but something major must have happened for a woman to treat her own daughter's children in such a callous, unequivocal way.

Years later, I asked my other granny whether she knew anything about this. She never named my mum; *her* was the best she could do. I didn't get much information, just a pursing of the lips, as she muttered, 'I blame *her* for everything.'

I didn't. I knew who was to blame for a whole lot more.

On another occasion at my granny's, my dad's sister Karen came in.

'I didn't know Valerie's bairns were here.'

'You won't raise *her* name in my house,' Granny retorted. 'She's a cow that one, always has been, always will be.'

'Call her by her name, for God's sake,' said Auntie Karen. 'It won't kill you. She's Harry's wife after all, wee Tracy and Gary are their kids.'

'Aye, Tracy, fair enough,' Granny replied. 'But Gary? I doubt it.'

My granny always said that my dad wasn't Gary's dad. They certainly looked nothing like each other, but that didn't make sense to me then, and it still doesn't. If Gary wasn't my dad's biological child and I was, then why was I the one he hated? Surely he must have hated me to do those things to me? Maybe Mum would feel more protective of the child who was a bastard – she had definitely been pregnant when they got married as I found out from birth and marriage certificates – and perhaps she even felt grateful to the man who had taken on another man's child, but why did she feel no love for me?

This then, this lack of love and surfeit of bitterness, was the background to my childhood; a dad who abused me and a mum who seemed incapable of showing me any affection whatsoever.

I had no one.

I was completely and utterly alone.

CHAPTER 8

ON THE OUTSIDE

I've never made that many friends – partly because of what was done to me, which made me withdrawn and wary, but also partly because of the life we led. In fact, I've probably only had about six really good friends over the course of my whole life. That's not to say I wouldn't have liked things to be different, but when your childhood is characterised by abuse, it turns everything on its head. I didn't know what normal was.

I think British kids on bases have a certain attitude to them – maybe it's changed now, but back then they were all very blasé. They never thought of friendships as long term, so it was always about who fitted in at that time. I was withdrawn anyway, but after the abuse began I would become even more so – partly this was because Dad was isolating me, but partly it was because I didn't have a maternal figure in my life.

Over the next three years, Mum would be in and out of hospital constantly. Her symptoms were baffling the medical experts and they couldn't understand why she would get flare-ups of her condition to begin with. There seemed to be no common denominator so they could never predict when she would be ill. Neither could we. It was many, many years later that she finally got a diagnosis – the condition was so rare it was no wonder they had been unable to pin it down.

When Mum was in hospital, Dad never looked after me. That probably seems a ridiculous statement given that I've already outlined such appalling abuse but, actually, I can't understand why his other actions were so neglectful. Given that he knew what he was doing was wrong, on every level, and given that he would have been torn limb from limb by others on the camp if they had found out that he was a paedophile, I would have thought he would have tried with all his might to deflect attention from us. One way of doing that would have been to ensure that we always fitted in, but, when Mum was away, I was uncared for. He was always telling me that I was the woman of the house, that household duties were my responsibility, but I was just a little kid. From being a child one moment, I was suddenly thrust into a situation whereby I wasn't just being violated, I was also having to run a home.

I couldn't do it. I actually, physically, couldn't do it. In the 1960s, life on an Army base wasn't one of unimaginable luxury. My dad had obviously lied to Agnes when he said he was getting someone in to help look after us while Mum was in hospital, but I wish he had – and not just for the obvious reason. Perhaps he wouldn't have had the same opportunities to abuse me (although I think that was so ingrained in who he was that he would always have found a way), but it would also have addressed the fact that I quickly became neglected. When Mum was admitted to hospital any time, Dad didn't look after me at all. He would never accept help from the neighbours when she was taken ill, and Agnes was not the only one to offer.

It was also Army practice to offer help in situations like ours. If Dad had been willing, there would have been a whole raft of help for us. I do remember that, on a few occasions, they sent a family liaison officer to see what they could provide, but my dad let them stay for about five minutes and said everything was fine. He lied that one of Mum's friends was helping out as well as making a big song and dance about not wanting to put anyone to any trouble – all of it adding to the accepted view of him as a great guy. The Army would have helped with practical things like shopping and washing, but that would not have fallen in line with Dad's plans at all. Not only was he trying to maintain the fiction of himself as a strong man coping with his family responsibilities in times of adversity, but he also needed to use these household chores to punish me.

I was very quickly pushed into housework, including such things as cooking, and got most of it wrong – I tended to burn toast, burn sausages, burn everything really. If it couldn't be burned, I had a talent for making it under-cooked. But it was when he told me I needed to do the washing that I really got into trouble because I just couldn't physically manage. He didn't tell me to wash his clothes – he couldn't run that risk. If he had gone to work in a smelly, damp uniform someone would have noticed or, at the very least, he would have been embarrassed by the smell. But that wasn't a consideration for my things.

We had an old-fashioned twin tub and a big communal garden with washing ropes to hang the laundry on. Needless to say, Dad didn't want me to use the garden as that would have meant me coming into contact with people and talking to them, so I had to dry everything indoors. I'd fill one barrel of the twin-tub with clothes and then have to drag them out and put them into the other side when they were sodding wet. It was physically hard, and I then had to dry them in the house. They were usually dripping wet when I hung them up on the clothes horse or on doors, and there was always a fusty, damp stink clinging to them.

When I put my school uniform on, it never smelled clean and I soon got called names by the other kids. This happened for the first time when Mum went into hospital and Dad started touching me, and even though she was only gone for a week at that point, he had asked me to wash my things. I could have got away with wearing them all week, and the smell would have been less than the stench I ended up with from the dampness. Perhaps this was a deliberate ploy of his, perhaps he was already working out ways to make sure I was an outsider and had no one to confide in. As soon as the other kids started calling me smelly, I was left to sit alone. It doesn't take long for children to work out who is the weakest in the pack. I also had to wash my own bed sheets, although Dad took his to the laundry in the Army mess, so I was never really in anything clean and always felt like an outsider.

As time went on and Mum's hospitalisations became more frequent, I would get more and more unkempt. My hair was long and it was rarely brushed. I couldn't reach all of it myself, and after Dad started watching me in the bath, I never voluntarily got in there or lingered. Hair washing was one of the first things to be sacrificed as I looked for ways to keep out of situations where I felt even more vulnerable. As a result, my hair smelled even worse than my clothes. The stink of his cigarettes seemed to linger and I couldn't get away from the constant reminder of him. I had to wash Gary's things too, and although he smelled just as much in terms of his school uniform, he had a double-edged attack to get round it – he smothered himself in Dad's Old Spice and also threatened to batter anyone who called him names. I wish my big brother had stuck up for me too.

I got to the stage where I couldn't smell myself any more. When we went on the bus to Rheindalen to go swimming, it would take ages to get there and that meant I'd have to endure what seemed like hours of people sniggering, throwing things at me and making fun of Smelly Tracy. It was a lonely life. I'm not saying for one minute that I was abused every day. Sometimes now I read the stories of other people and think they couldn't possibly have survived what they say happened to them as little children. No, it wasn't constant, but there were precious few glimmers of light in there. Even when I wasn't being used as my father's plaything, it was just a miserable existence.

It sounds absolutely ghastly, but the only time I was ever given any affection was when Dad was abusing me. After he had been doing those awful things to me for about a year, maybe slightly more, he also started using endearments when he did things – I was still a dirty little bitch, but he would also call me 'doll' and 'sweetheart'. Did he say these things to convince himself that it was all fine, that our perverted relationship was actually 'normal'? I don't know, but I do know it was the only time I ever had any nice words spoken to me.

Mum made it quite clear that I was little more than a nuisance. If I was upset about little childhood things, she would tell me to stop being such a bother. She'd make comments such as 'I suppose I'll have to clean that up', if I scraped my knee. I once cut my hand quite badly and my request for a plaster was met with, 'God, do you ever stop asking for things?' Gary would play-act a lot; he'd trip over his own feet, fall down and scream that he'd broken his back, and Mum would come running as if her life depended on it. He never did hurt himself, but she was always there to console her boy, always there to make it better. She treated me differently for all of those years. I loved her so much when we lived in Germany and kept striving for her to love me back, but there was never anything to hold on to.

Even my dad, even the man abusing me, noticed what she was like. He would often have to be careful with how he made me accept the abuse if he had seen my mum being particularly cold with me. He stuck to saying we had to keep it a secret, that we couldn't let anyone know because then she wouldn't get better. Yet he was probably wondering himself just how long he could get away with getting me to accept violations for a woman who would barely give me the time of day. She didn't hate me, she just didn't seem to be bothered. Now that I too am a mother, I can see how odd she was; I lived in eternal hope that she would love me, or even notice me and show me a few small kindnesses.

My love for, and attachment to, her was unwavering, as is the love of many children for undeserving parents, and without it my dad would never have got away with what he did. Mum's detachment from me meant she wasn't even bothered about other aspects of my care. While Gary got everything new, I was given his hand-me-downs, such as school jumpers, socks and vests, or taken to the second-hand stores. Even then she was miserable in my company. My dad gave her a budget for our clothing, and she spent it all, bar a few Deutschmarks, on Gary. The other kids saw this, picked on me, and I reacted not in anger, but with emotional detachment of the sort my mother was so good at. Maybe it was genetic. You close off, close down, when you're in the middle of a life like that, but I never really knew anything that was different. I do remember looking at other little girls one day when we were trawling round charity shops looking for shoes for me. I was being dragged along and she was telling me to 'stop being so bloody slow', while these other girls were having a nice time with their mummies, walking together, swinging their arms, being friends. I guess I just saw our relationship as something to be accepted. That's the way she was. When, in my adult-hood, I asked her why she was like that, she just shrugged and said it was her illness – maybe it was. I'm sure her condition was awful for her, but she managed to be different with Gary.

We stayed in Rinteln until 1970, when I was eight, and I was abused throughout those years. Actually, 'abuse' isn't a word that was used in those days by many people, and at the time it wasn't something I applied to my own situation, but, as people have become more aware of what happens to many children and as those children have spoken out, the term has become much more accepted. I use it now, because it is clearly what happened, but in those days, if it was spoken of at all in public, adults would refer to it using words such as 'fiddling' and 'interfering', terms which underestimate and minimise devastating attacks on young people which should never be hidden.

But mine was hidden, and I didn't even have words to describe it back then – I barely knew what was happening, just that I hated and dreaded it. Of course I've wondered if my mum knew what was going on, but I realise that it's hard to analyse the past. I remember on many occasions saying to Dad, 'Mum doesn't love me,' and his reply was always the same. 'She'll love you more if you do this.' Everything I said about her was linked to another excuse for him to do things to me; he never missed a trick. 'If you do this, she'll love you,' he'd say, or, 'If you keep doing these things, she'll start to love you, but if you stop, she won't.'

She never did. She never gave me a squirt of her perfume or little presents. I can actually remember the specifics of the times she was nice to me – once, she put the Avon lavender shoe soaps in my bedroom, and once she gave me a purse with 20p in it.

For Christmas and birthdays, I got mostly practical presents, clothes and educational books once I was at school. I tended to get one playful present at Christmas and the rest would be things such as a three-pack of socks, which was expected to last all year (with Gary's being given to me when that didn't happen) and two pairs of pants. I was once given a ready-reckoner-type machine for spelling where the words came out at the top and you had to see how quickly you could read them and spell them back again. My father kept saying to Mum, 'She needs education, she doesn't need toys,' and she accepted his word unquestioningly, so they have to share the blame really.

There was a toy cupboard in our house, but it was Gary's really as I didn't have much to put in there. His side was crammed with cars and soldiers and boy things, but mine was sparse. I had a kaleidoscope, a golliwog that had travelled with me from when we had been based in Singapore, and a three-foot-tall walking doll. When I got the doll, the first thing I did was strip it completely, including the knickers. I was sitting in the living room doing that one Christmas when my dad came in. He went ballistic but had to keep his voice down as he didn't want to draw attention to what I was doing. 'What the fuck are you up to?' he whispered in an angry voice, trying to avoid Mum or Gary hearing him from the kitchen. 'Get the clothes back on that fucking doll, you little weirdo.'

'I just wanted to look, Dad,' I told him.

'Well, don't. It's none of your fucking business.'

The irony wasn't lost on me even at that age. I couldn't look at a naked doll, but I could engage in sex acts with my own father. I had just been curious. I wanted to see what my dolly had inside her pants, I wanted to see if she was the same as me. There was a part of me which was keen to see what she had down there that was so fascinating. If my dad couldn't keep his hands off me and was always taking my pants off, I wanted to know what there was that he was drawn to, and I naively thought I would be able to see that in a doll.

The next Christmas I was given a Barbie and I hadn't learned my lesson. As soon as my mum and Gary left the room – I think they had gone to see Agnes to wish her a Merry Christmas – I ripped her clothes off and turned her upside down to look at what was between her legs. My dad was sitting on his chair, drinking as usual, and he was watching me quietly this time. I was amazed by bodies. Every doll I saw drew me in and I wanted to have a closer look.

'You've been told about that,' he said, eventually. 'Stop being so fucking strange. Play with your fucking dolls, don't poke about at them.'

I ignored him – I was rarely defiant at that stage, but it was Christmas and, given that he wasn't actually shouting at me, I thought it was worth chancing my luck.

'Do you fucking hear me?' he asked. He stormed over to where I was sitting on the floor and grabbed the Barbie out of my hands. 'Give her back!' I shouted. I'd only just been given my pretty doll and didn't want him to confiscate it already. 'Please! I'll be good! Please give her back, Daddy!' I begged.

'No fucking chance,' he sneered, and threw her into the fire. I couldn't help myself – I screamed. As I watched my lovely new present – the only decent thing I'd been given that year – melting in the flames, Mum came in. 'What's going on here?' she asked.

My dad looked at me, and I could see the warning in his eyes. 'Tracy's been stupid – she was having a tantrum, throwing her doll about, and she dropped it in the fire.'

'Tracy!' Mum exclaimed. 'Oh, for goodness' sake! That's just typical of you – you're such an annoying little girl.' She stamped out of the room and my dad smiled. 'You've upset your mum, Tracy. She chose that doll for you.'

'But it was you, Dad . . .' I started to say, but he cut me off.

'No. No, it was you, Tracy. Your fault. And now, now your mum is very upset. You'll have to make it up to her, won't you?'

I nodded, the tears running down my cheeks. This was so unfair, but I knew I couldn't fight. He always won.

'I'll go and say sorry,' I said to him.

'No, no, don't do that. I'll tell her – but, Tracy? You're going to have to be a very, very good girl to make up for this. Do you understand?'

By this time, I understood. I understood only too well.

CHAPTER 9

SAVING MUM

The families on the base lived on streets which were about a mile long each. There were always lots of people about and the area was quite large, but I kept myself to myself. After the abuse began, Dad was keen to keep me indoors as much as possible (although Gary was allowed much more freedom), so even if I had wanted to mix, I didn't really have the opportunity.

It was strange the way in which my new life acquired a pattern so quickly. I would say that, within six months, everything had been turned upside down. Dad wasn't trying to hide his anger nearly as much as he had to start with. When Mum had been hospitalised on the night of the storm, he had become violent and verbally abusive the very next day, but when she came back from being an in-patient, he didn't swear at me around her or hit me when she was present. However, as time went on, and her periods in hospital became more and more frequent, he gained confidence in being the man he wanted to be – perhaps the man he had *always* wanted to be. He would swear at me in front of Mum, and although he saved particular words for when he was sexually abusing me, he wasn't shy about telling me to 'move my arse' or 'stop being so fucking lazy'. Mum raised her eyebrows at him a few times to begin with, but I suppose she had more to contend with given the unpredictability of her health. Dad had also started to give me the odd backhander when she was around – which increased in frequency throughout the next six months.

All I can think now, is that once Mum started going into hospital more, and as her illness got more severe, she was more dependent on him than ever and so he could really stamp his authority on the household. He tried little things at a time, a swear word here and there, a slap to me every now and again – when he got away with it, he tried a little more the next day. Mum never stood up for me. He never hit her, though, and on the one occasion when she did see him give Gary a whack, she hit the roof. It happened about four months after her first hospital admission; she had already been back in a few times. Dad was in the kitchen making a cup of tea – a rare occurrence in itself – and Gary came in. He pushed past my dad as he was reaching for a snack. Dad's hand came out automatically – he probably thought it was me – and he whacked him across the cheek. Mum, who had been in the living room, appeared in a flash as Gary cried out.

'Never do that again!' she exclaimed. 'You never, EVER lift a finger to him! Do you hear me?' she shrieked.

My dad could do nothing but nod.

'Not him,' she said. 'You don't touch him.'

The message couldn't have been clearer had she spelled it out in flashing lights. I could be slapped whenever my dad's fancy kicked in. I was fair game, but Gary was protected. I certainly never saw my dad hit him again. On that afternoon, Mum took Gary back through to the living room, leading him by the hand as if he had just been battered to within an inch of his life. Gary played on it, and they sat wrapped up together for the rest of the day while my dad shouted at, and threatened me, as compensation.

Mum was always kind to Gary, she had all the time in the world for him, but I was pretty much invisible. This is what my dad played on in particular. Every time he touched me, every time his hands and fingers went places they shouldn't, he would whisper to me, 'Good girl, you're doing this for your mum, and this will help to keep her out of hospital, won't it?' It was our little secret, it was what he used to keep me in line, but he was also fully aware that I was desperate for Mum to notice me. If he could convince me that the abuse was a way of making her well again, then surely she would be grateful to me?

One day, Agnes came round while Mum was at a hospital appointment. Dad opened the door – I would never have been brave enough to do that on my own as I was under strict instructions to keep away from everyone – and she saw me cowering behind him as she asked after my mum. 'Hiya, Tracy,' she said, 'I was just saying to your dad that the doctors will take good care of Valerie. They'll do their best to make her well again.'

I smiled – but I knew she was wrong. It wasn't down to the doctors, it was down to me. If I kept being a good girl Mum would get better. When Dad closed the door to Agnes, he confirmed what I had been thinking. 'She doesn't know what she's talking about,' he said. 'You know what you need to do, don't you, Tracy? You know how to keep your mum out of hospital?' I nodded as he motioned for me to go into his bedroom. He called out to Gary to bull his boots, telling him not to stop until he was told, and made some excuse about helping me with my homework. Yet again, I was placed back in the personal hell he had created for me.

This was the circle of abuse he maintained and developed. I was always kept next door to my dad's bedroom wherever we lived. He isolated me from friends and neighbours. He used key words to let me know what was happening without being explicit. I was his *good girl.* We had *fun.* It was time to *make Mum well again.* And the thing was, he was very clever. He timed the abuse perfectly – of course, now I know he had access to things I never thought of, he would know what the doctors were telling Mum, he would be fully aware of when she was getting worse or better, or when she was due to go into hospital for a few days. He put all of this together and made me believe it was all down to me. My behaviour, my collusion in the abuse, was what determined my mum's health according to him – and how could a five-year-old challenge that?

One Saturday, when the house was empty and I wasn't at

school, Mum and Gary left for the afternoon, her to get some shopping at the NAAFI, him to play with his friends. I tried to sneak into my room after the door closed but Dad called on me within seconds.

'Get through here!' he shouted. He only ever seemed to be shouting at me these days – actually, that wasn't quite right, but the other times, when he didn't shout, were the times I didn't want to think about.

I never challenged him back then. I trotted meekly through to where he sat, on 'his' chair as always, the stench of beer and fag smoke surrounding him. 'Your mum's gone out,' he said. I knew that. 'Gary's out too.' I knew that as well. He narrowed his eyes at me as if focusing on what was standing in front of him. 'It's just you and me.' He paused. 'I hope you're going to be a good girl, Tracy, because, I have to tell you, your mum hasn't been feeling too good lately.' I remember thinking that I hadn't noticed her being sick or complaining of things going wrong again. Of course, I was still believing his lies and thinking I had some control over Mum's health, but he, as always, was spinning a web of lies. 'So, it's important that we – that *you* – do everything you can to change that.'

I knew what was coming – or I thought I did – but I really, really didn't want to suffer any of that again, so I breathed deeply and said the words I suspected would make him blow his top.

'Daddy,' I whispered, 'I don't really want to do the things that you said we have to do.'

His reaction surprised me. He didn't shout. He didn't

81

clout me. He just narrowed his eyes still further and leaned towards me as I stood in front of him. 'Do you *want* your mum to be sick, Tracy?'

I shook my head.

'Why are you such a bad girl? Why do you only think of yourself? You know that you are the one who can make mum better, who can stop her ever having to go into hospital again, don't you? And you know that if she does go into hospital, you're to blame.'

I was so confused. I wanted to be good, but why couldn't I do other things to be a good girl? I wanted Mum to stay well, but I wanted someone else to be able to save her.

'Now, come here, come closer – and, for fuck's sake, Tracy, think of someone other than yourself for once.' He grabbed me by the wrist and pulled me to him, his tone of voice changing instantly. 'Your mother is a very ill woman, and it's your job to make sure she gets better.' He calmed down a little before his next words. 'You'd like her to be well, I know you would, and you *can* be a good girl when you try. So, here's what we'll try, come here.'

He pulled me onto the chair beside him, never once letting go of my hand. He unzipped his trousers as he sat there, and I thought he was going to start touching me while he did those odd things to himself – but, no. This was even worse. He wanted me to touch him *there*.

He guided my hand towards his pants where, thankfully, he was still covered up. 'There you go, Tracy, touch that. Go on, be a good girl.' He forced my hand onto his penis; I was so little and so weak compared to him there was no way I could physically resist him, but I did have enough disgust to say, 'No, Dad, no, I don't want to.'

'Well, you fucking will,' he retorted. With that, he pushed my hand inside his pants. I was so shocked to feel him – I knew, just as he shouldn't touch me in private parts, I shouldn't touch him, but what could I do? He had pushed himself against me before and masturbated right next to me – on me, on many occasions – but this was something a step further, and it was grotesque.

I had no idea what to do, but he made sure that I did what he needed. He uncurled my fingers and wrapped them around him, holding me in place, and then moved my hand up and down. As always, he stared at me constantly and, as always, the insults flew as soon as he started to get excited. 'You like that, don't you? You're a dirty little bitch really, aren't you?' he would say, as I could do no more than weep while he manipulated my hand back and forth. 'Pretending that you don't want to; you know exactly what you're doing, don't you? You love doing this, don't you, filthy little bitch.'

I tried to block it all out, but my hand was getting so sore. Just as I thought I could go on no longer, it stopped. A horrible warm wetness covered my hand and my dad relaxed against the back of his chair. I was at a loss. What now? I should have known that the next stage of his abuse of me would continue as it usually did. He lay there for a few moments then looked down at my hand lying across his lap.

'Get off me! Get to the fucking bathroom now and wash yourself, you're disgusting,' he snapped. I did as I was told, holding my hand out in front as if it was infected, and the same old routine continued with me washing, him watching, and both of us knowing it would happen again very soon.

No one seemed to pick him up on anything. When I went to school in filthy clothes, with matted hair and a stench of neglect, the teachers said nothing. Other children were quick to pick up on it, but the adults kept quiet. I would have thought that a child who had gone from being reasonably well looked after to one in the state I was would have elicited some comment or some concern, but there was nothing. When Mum got back from hospital, some things changed a little, but each time she returned to be an inpatient, or each time she was too unwell to do anything, it all slipped again. If I was dirty and unkempt when she got home, she said nothing. If she felt better, she'd give me a bath, but I was so terrified by that time of even being in the bathroom that I used every excuse I could think of to avoid it. When she wasn't there and Dad made me wash in front of him, that was about the only time I saw soap and water.

Not only did these things mark me out as different, but I smelled of him. He was always touching me, rubbing himself on me, masturbating on me or close to me, and that in itself had a horrible odour. Even when he wasn't there, he left me with those memories. Perhaps I shouldn't have been so surprised that no one said anything because, as time went on, I would try to draw even more attention to myself, through smoking and bad behaviour, through truancy and vandalism, but the attitude among adults always seemed to be one of ignoring as much as possible. It breaks my heart even to this day when I hear of children being labelled 'bad' because of their behaviour. I always wonder what's behind it as I don't believe any child is that way naturally – they are generally acting out what has happened to them and been done to them by adults.

From the age of five, when Dad started on me, I became much more aware of Mum's illness, because I now believed I was responsible for her. I started to listen out for the sounds of her vomiting, and I looked for the tell-tale lumps and boils on her skin. If she had abscesses, I was concerned, if she said she felt dizzy, I panicked. Was she going to have to go back to hospital because I wasn't letting him touch me enough, I wondered? Was she going to get even more unwell because I hadn't touched him when he asked me to?

This was my overriding concern almost every waking moment. I never knew when I was to be abused, because Dad would vary the situation. There would be times when everything would be in place but he wouldn't touch me – even when Mum was at bingo, or the NAAFI, and Gary was playing in a football match, he would sometimes leave me alone. However, on those occasions, when I was left with no one but him, I shook with fear from the moment the door closed behind Mum and Gary. He would be sitting in the living room, drinking and smoking, and I'd be in my room – waiting. He would often shout through, 'That's the house empty now, Tracy,' as if to warn me that, any moment, he might ask me to come through to him, but there were times that he seemed to just use those occasions to taunt me. I would spend two or three hours awaiting my fate, knowing it was entirely up to him.

Can you imagine what that does to a child? There were times when I almost willed him to get it over with, and that is unforgivable. What sort of man, what sort of father, has his five-year-old daughter in such a state of fear that she almost wants him to begin the abuse so she will at least know there will be an end to it for that day? Perhaps that was just another way for him to get his perverted kicks. Almost every instance of abuse involved him also telling me that I liked it, that I enjoyed it, that I was a dirty little bitch who wanted it, so I don't think he gained sexual pleasure during the times he violated me from my fear alone. I certainly think that was another aspect of his character at other times, such as when he teased me about whether it would happen that day or not, so there is a chance that he was conditioning me to be entirely compliant. If I had turned into his nasty, paedophilic dream and become willing to engage in his horrors, maybe I would have been hit less, maybe I would have suffered less verbal abuse – but I couldn't do it; the times when I almost wished for it to begin so it would be over as soon as possible left me feeling even worse.

I would suffer through it all. I'd bear it for my mum. But I would never want these horrible things. At that stage, and up until I was about eight, I would always wonder what he would do to me each time. No matter his chosen form of abuse, each one had its own horrors. When he touched me in places that were so private, I felt so ashamed. I knew it was wrong, that a daddy shouldn't do these things, but it was also very painful. I was only little, and he wasn't gentle. His nasty, grown-up hands and fingers went to parts of me that should never have been violated – afterwards, it would be hard for me to go to the toilet and sometimes to walk.

On the occasions when he touched himself to the point of orgasm beside me, I would feel sick at the smell. I had no idea what it was, but I finally realised that he must want that vile sticky stuff to come out of his private parts because he seemed to calm down afterwards. While it was going on, his face was terribly contorted and I would wonder if he was unwell – as he did it more and more, I eventually realised this was just part of it. He had to make these funny faces and funny noises for the sticky stuff to come out. He would touch me with one hand while he did that, and touch himself with the other. If I screwed my face up or gagged, or gave any indication that I didn't want to be there, he would release one hand to slap me or punch me in the kidneys, before going back to what he was doing.

These were ghastly 'activities' and I hated them with all my heart, but the worst was when he made me touch him. Since the first time he had forced that on me, it had haunted me and I dreaded it beyond everything else. As time went on, he would find even more horrors to inflict on me and I took it all, all to save my mum.

CHAPTER 10

RESPECT

He had a face for everyone. I don't have to say again what he was to me, but I'm sure the neighbours and everyone on the base thought he was a martyr for looking after us whenever Mum was unwell. Men always get more credit for that than women do, and in those days it was even more unusual for a dad to take care of his kids, even though the reality was that I really wasn't being looked after at all. By the time I was eight, and the abuse had been going on for three years, he was explicit about my role in his life.

He had started coming into my room to abuse me the year before. Now that my own personal space had been violated as much as my body, I had no safe area in which to disappear. He could get me anywhere – I was fair game in any room of the house. I could barely remember a time when this hadn't been happening. In fact, I had always had a strange feeling that something wasn't quite right in my life and remember how I used to hide in the cellar when we lived on another base. I recalled that one of the caretakers on the base found me one time and I was sobbing when he took me back home, but I wasn't quite sure why.

In all truth, I have no idea whether I was abused before we moved to Germany. My dad's character had seemingly changed so quickly and so markedly on that first night when my mum was taken into hospital, but I wonder sometimes whether that had actually been the starting point or whether there was more that even I couldn't bring to the front of my mind.

Nothing seemed to inspire my dad. Apart from reading his spy books and cowboy stories, he did little else. He was drinking a lot through these years. That didn't excuse what he did, but it must have had an effect on his mood, and perhaps he used it to make it easier in some ways for him to do what he did. I almost hope so – I hope he needed some anaesthetic for what he did to me. I wish I'd had something. He would meet other soldiers in the halfway house, the pub they all frequented nearby. The pub had a German name but everyone called it the halfway house as it was halfway between the camp and the town. He was definitely different with them and they all would say what a great guy he was; it was just another aspect of his split personality.

Sometimes Gary and I were allowed to meet him in the taproom when it was time for him to walk home. Gary had been allowed to do this much more than I had, as I guess Dad would have worried about me even coming to somewhere of his choosing as there were too many chances for me to meet someone along the way and get chatting. By the time I was allowed, I was in such fear of him and so worried about my disobedience putting Mum back in hospital if I ever said 'no' that he felt safe enough letting me out. The first time I walked into the taproom, it seemed overpowering. It was loud and smelled of beer – a stench I hated as I associated it with my dad hurting me. There was a lot of laughter and people seemed to be happy, but that was alien to me.

Dad was sitting near the door with friends and I saw him as soon as I went in. He waved me over, unsmiling, and I stood next to him at the end of the table. Back then, when I noticed how these other men were with him, I didn't know the appropriate word to use to describe the relationship they seemed to have and their attitude towards him. It came to me some years later – respectful. They were extremely respectful towards Dad. In fact, they were like that with each other too, but even more so with him. Around them were just the normal sounds of groups of blokes winding down after a difficult day at work. They'd be laughing and joking, sometimes singing, but always good-natured. It was different at my dad's table that night, and every other night I went for him.

'Stand there,' he said when I walked up to the table. 'This is my daughter, Tracy,' he told the others. I thought that was quite strange – they obviously knew him, and they must have all known who lived where and what sort of families they had, but he was being very formal. None of the other men even said hello. I could hear all the noise from the rest of the pub, but it was as if everything was silent at that table. After what seemed like ages, he took his coat from the back of the chair and said, 'Right, let's go.'

All of the men got up and put their jackets on too. They shook hands with each other, and no one was missed out. There were no slaps on the back, no camaraderie. Dad pushed me back towards the door and we walked home in silence. It was very peculiar. When I told a friend about this as an adult, she asked whether my dad had been in the Masons. I have considered that, but, if he was, he never mentioned it, nor did he ever seem to go to meetings, wear Masonic regalia, or even have anything good going on in his life which might have suggested he knew people in the right places.

No, the real reason was, I believe, much more sinister.

He was showing me to other men who had the same depraved needs as he did.

I'm not imagining that, and what happened on other occasions adds more evidence to my understanding of the situation. Every time I saw Dad with these friends, every time I went to the taproom for him, they were the same people. They sat away from everyone else; no other soldiers approached their table. There were no laughs; there was no sense of fun. They kept their voices down and they always had that formal approach to each member of their group.

The weekend after I met him in the halfway house for the first time, he had to work on the Saturday morning. This often happened. On this occasion, he woke me up early. 'Get up and get dressed,' he snapped. 'You're coming to work with me.' I did as I was told. As we walked to his office, the only conversation we had was when he told me how to behave.

'If anyone comes in, keep quiet. Speak if you're spoken to, but keep it short and sweet,' he instructed.

There was a steady stream of other personnel coming in, and I didn't have any concerns about any of them. They were friendly to me and most of them would say, 'Who's this you've got in with you today then?' Dad wouldn't elaborate at all. He'd simply say, 'My daughter, Tracy,' and answer their question or give them what they needed. I'd smile shyly, but say nothing, wary of how he had told me to behave. Quite often, other clerks would come in, and they were all nice to me. There was, again, a lot of respect shown to him. No one was there for small chat exactly, but he would just coldly give them what they needed and hurry them out.

Until one man came in. I thought I recognised him from the halfway house, but I couldn't be sure, given that no one really engaged with me there either. He didn't ask who I was, but my dad said to him immediately, 'This is Tracy.'

The man nodded.

All I remember is that they said a few inconsequential things to each other, along the lines of 'everything all right?' and comments like that.

Nothing else happened that day, and I went with my dad for a few weekends after that and the same things happened. He stopped working on Saturdays and Sundays after a while, and started to go on exercise instead. Exercises were compulsory and happened at least twice a year. The men would go away from their families. All or most of the camp would go, usually for a week or two, and at least once a year they had a long one which lasted between four and six weeks. Dad was exempt from most of these because of Mum's illness but at times he seemed to opt back in – I think he didn't like them because of his laziness more than anything, and I suspect he was shown up by the real soldiers when he went on them. I was surprised when he started going on them. After a few weeks, he told me that help was needed in the kitchen and that he'd volunteered me. I was still too young for that sort of thing really, but as I'd been doing so much around the house for so many years now, it didn't surprise me.

When we got there, he didn't go off with the others; he took me into the kitchen. We were the only ones there early on and he started explaining things to me. There was an old toasting machine, the sort where you place the split rolls on a tray and they roll through, getting toasted on the way before they drop off the end. I was told to do hamburgers that way too, four at a time. It was quite a small place, maybe about eight feet long and just wide enough for someone to stand at the toasting machine with no one behind them. The mess itself had a huge kitchen, but this area was really just for making snacks. Given the way it was laid out, I was squashed almost in a corner making the rolls as other people came in, some to get the hot drinks ready, others to grab something to eat. People said 'hello' or mentioned how nice it was for me to help out, but Dad had already given me his usual speech about not engaging with others, so I didn't chat.

He was standing on the other side of the partition where we handed food through when I heard someone say,

'Where's Tracy?' I didn't know anyone, so couldn't imagine why there would be a man asking for me by name. I didn't hear my father replying to him, but seconds later a burly chap came in and headed straight for me. I was still standing over the toasting machine and he walked over behind me, squeezing past everyone else.

'Hello there, young Tracy,' he said, smiling.

I said 'hello' back to him, and kept my head down as I made the burgers. I suspected Dad was somewhere nearby and I didn't want to get into trouble for talking – not that I particularly wanted to talk to this man anyway.

'Busy?' he asked as he moved closer. I looked behind me at him and said nothing. He was very close to me. There wasn't much space where I was working anyway, but he had chosen to put himself there. As I moved the burgers and bread rolls through the machine, he pushed the front of his body into the back of mine. It was like the situation when Dad made me change the duvet cover all over again. I had no idea what to do – if I drew attention to what was happening I feared I would get into trouble. All the things Dad regularly called me, all the blame he laid on me for what happened, went through my mind. The kitchen was busy and no one was paying attention to what was going on. This man was pressing hard into me and I knew what I could feel; I had felt Dad's often enough. He was getting harder and harder and he had a horrible grin on his face.

All of a sudden, I heard Dad call 'Graham!' from the door of the kitchen.

The man moved away from me, slapped me on the backside, and waved. 'Harry!' he called, walking towards him. 'Something wrong?'

My Dad didn't answer immediately. When he did, he just said, 'No, nothing's wrong – a word, if you don't mind?' Graham left the room with him and I continued making the food. I knew I couldn't get upset and I knew I had to keep going through the motions or there would be a few hard punches and slaps waiting for me when we got home.

Nothing was said by my father about what had happened, but I thought I knew. It came to me in a flash of realisation that they had been talking, he had been one of the men I had seen in the halfway house, and he had known my name. Dad had shown me to him, and he had thought he had the right to do what he did. What did that mean? Had Dad told other men what he was doing to me? If that was the case, did that mean they thought it was fine? If he had told them of the abuse and they hadn't told him he was a bad man, then all the things he had been indoctrinating me with were true – this was OK, this was what made me a good girl.

My head was spinning. If he was telling other people, did that mean men like Graham could do these things to me as well? Was that what he was trying? Was he paving the way?

What a horrible situation for a young child. Not only was I being violated by the person who should care for me, who should be my hero, but I was also now living in fear that it was going to be done by other men too. My horror that Dad was bragging about what he did and presenting me as an option to other men was compounded the next time we were at the mess and I was sent into the tiny kitchen again. I had told my dad that morning I didn't want to go, but he'd just laughed at me and told me to go and put my coat on.

I could hear him outside the kitchen talking to people, then I heard a man's voice say, quite loudly, 'Where's Tracy?' Just then a stranger walked towards me, leering, and made for the tiny space behind me just as Graham had done. As he walked over, I could see that he was already excited and I couldn't help myself shout out, 'Dad!' My father came into the kitchen and looked at this man, who, still smiling, shook his head and left. I was torn. What a position to be in – I'd had to ask for help from the man who abused me to stop another man from touching me, when I was pretty sure that he was the one telling them about me.

This was the pattern of my life – he was still doing what he did, and now I had to worry about others joining in. I think that, when I was very little, when it all started, I almost accepted it – it was my normality. However, as I got older, I began to wonder. I was meant to be Mum's saviour, but she was still getting ill. Why was that? Why was I putting up with what he did to me if it wasn't changing anything? He said she would get even worse if I wasn't a good girl, but I couldn't see how it could be worse. Mum didn't love me, she didn't even seem to like me, which sometimes made me think that we *should* tell her all I was doing to try and make her better, for maybe then she would care for me a little. Now, I was finding Dad's 'outside' behaviour odd too – and these men who he seemed to be showing me to, parading me in front of, gave me an uneasy feeling that I couldn't quite explain.

It was getting worse – but we were going to be on the move soon, and I could only hope that would mean a change in my life too.

CHAPTER 11

NORTHERN IRELAND

When it was announced we were moving, I was delighted. It wasn't presented as an option to Gary and me, it was a *fait accompli*. That we were going to Northern Ireland was even better in my mind – although I'd been born abroad, and although I'd lived most of my life on foreign bases, I still thought of myself as British. My parents both had strong Scottish accents, which I had picked up, so I was glad to be going somewhere I thought would feel more like home.

Dad was in a bad mood about it but it was what was called a 'natural' posting, just one of the moves all personnel had to deal with. As there was so much going on in Northern Ireland in the 1970s, pretty much every soldier had to do a tour of duty there – things were getting bad, with constant bombings and threats. Mum had been quite well for a while, but she was upset about the fact that Dad clearly didn't want to go. She asked if he could request somewhere else, but he said everyone had to do at least one tour there. I think there were three reasons for his reluctance – he didn't want to leave his buddies behind and he didn't want to break the hold he had over me by going somewhere new. However, above all of that, I think the main problem was that he was a coward. So many brave men and women lost their lives, or had their lives wrecked, during the Troubles but my father simply wasn't that sort of man. He was terrified at the very thought of being in such a dangerous environment. A lot of the kids had been there and come back to Germany again, so I knew how perilous it was. Children on Army bases talk about things like that all the time, it's their way of coping. The older ones said you could hear bombs and it was exciting, but, again, that was largely bravado. We had a sense of what it might be like but nothing could prepare us for how bad Northern Ireland in 1970 would be.

The set-up was the same wherever you went in those days – there were sometimes different colours, but the furniture was all the same. Everything was always dated. School was only a hundred metres down the road from where we lived, but there were lots of restrictions and barricades – and, of course, there were the same restrictions and barricades on my life at home. I don't think I really expected the abuse to stop; it was only the scenery which was changing. Dad was angry the whole time we were there. As soon as the others left the house, the swearing would start and the fury within him would lead to more sexual and physical attacks on me.

Outside, things were bad too. The political situation in Northern Ireland was something which obviously affected us all enormously, and yet, at the same time, we were protected to a large degree. Life inside the Army camp continued as it had in every other Army camp for years, but we knew there were events going on outside which restricted our movements and coloured our experiences.

Obviously, any child living in that sort of environment in any country feels its impact in some way, but we were the living embodiment of a government and political system hated by so many of those around us. When we went to school, we learned Irish history. When we passed by boarded-up shops and drove through barricades, we knew it was something to do with our country and we knew our dads were there to help people, but we were just kids — I can't remember any of us having political opinions and I can't remember my dad actually talking about the rights and wrongs of what was going on there. To this day, when I hear or read something about the Troubles, I find it hard to process that I was part of that time. I don't think that's simply because I had such awful things going on in my own life, I think it's because we were almost completely cocooned.

What I had learned in class was that the whole of Northern Ireland was unstable — there were some people who hated being called British, and there were some people who would fight until their dying breath for the privilege of being called the same thing. It all seemed very complicated. There was no talk in Army camps of peace campaigners and civil rights leaders — everything was black and white. Sinn Fein, the IRA, the RUC and internment were all words and phrases I heard, but they didn't mean much. In retrospect, I think that was partly because Dad wasn't on the front line. He wasn't a hero, he wasn't involved in peace-keeping or ensuring the safety of Irish people from either side – he was just a little man sitting in an office pretending he was one of the big boys. If he'd been out on the streets with his life in danger every day, maybe I'd have known more, but, as it was, the most information I got was from the TV, when I was allowed to watch it, and from school history lessons.

By the time we went to Northern Ireland, the violence was at fever pitch. The IRA had become much more powerful, and bombings were a way of life. People were being arrested and imprisoned without trial under internment, and a British accent was enough to put your life in danger if you walked the streets – which I was never allowed to do. No one could be trusted. I do remember Mum talking to another woman about the young girls who hung about the soldiers whenever they left the camp – I wondered whether they were as young as me and whether they were trying to help their mummies too. She made it clear that she blamed them for trying to 'trap' the soldiers, and when I heard her talking about 'prostitutes' I was very confused. Were these girls like me? I wondered about the word because that's what my dad now called me and the word itself wasn't one I knew the real meaning of. His use of that had only started in Northern Ireland. One night, when my mum was at bingo as usual, he had been touching me in bed. As he forced me to masturbate him, a sly smile crossed his face and stopped his frantic breathing for a moment. 'Do you know what you are?' he'd said, not waiting for my response. 'You're a right little prostitute. Aren't you? You love all of this, don't you? You're a little prostitute. You're my little prostitute.'

I was ten years old.

When my mum referred to these women and used the same word, I tried to work out what she meant. What was there that made us the same, I wondered?

One day, in class, we were being taught Irish history. The teacher asked us if we knew anything about Catholics and Protestants. Desperate to do well, I put my hand up.

'Tracy,' she said, smiling. 'What do you know?'

'I'm one,' I said, happily. 'I'm a prostitute.'

She frowned at me. 'A Protestant. That's what you mean.'

'No, I'm a prostitute. That's what my dad calls me.'

It was the first time I had said anything in public which could have raised suspicions, but I had thought it was fine to bring it up, reasoning that if the teacher had said the word, it must be OK. She shook her head, presumably dismissing it as something I'd misheard, and went back to the lesson. It would have been funny if it wasn't so sad.

Now we had moved from Germany, I did hope that perhaps I might be given a bit more freedom – I thought I had shown Dad he could trust me as I hadn't told anyone about our 'secret'. While I had been given plenty of new warnings about the threats in Northern Ireland, my concerns were closer to home. I didn't want to go wandering around the whole country, I just wanted to get out of the house, play, and maybe make some friends. I noticed very soon after we arrived that there was another girl who used to sit outside her house playing on her own. Her family lived directly opposite and I could see her from my bedroom window. She looked about ten or eleven, and I really hoped we could be friends. I saw something sad in her, her whole demeanour seemed shy and I wondered whether I might finally have someone I could talk to.

It didn't take long for things at home to fall into the same routine as in Germany. Mum was ill sometimes, but didn't have to go into hospital, and there was still a lot of shouting in the house, most of it directed at me. It seemed as if Dad was getting more and more openly angry at me, and I can only think, in retrospect, that was part of his plan to try and make me seem like a terrible child. If he did this, Mum would presumably have no time for any 'stories' I then chose to tell her, and everyone would just think I was spouting lies as part of my 'badness'.

Dad seemed unhappy in Northern Ireland. I don't see how it could have been as a result of his job, because he wasn't in any danger. While there were many brave soldiers walking the streets and risking life and limb every day, he was in an office doing very little. He never left the base for work, so wasn't risking anything happening to him as part of the Troubles. What had changed in his life were two things – he had to re-establish the controls over me which he had in place while we were in Germany, part of which depended on my mum making new friends, and he was away from the group of men he was so close to back in the other camp. His personality seemed to change wherever he was posted, and he was very morose this time, with a lack of confidence. The only thing which remained the same and which gave his ego a boost was that he could still abuse a child. That was his rock.

He needn't have worried about Mum. As an Army wife of many years, she always had new friends, and there was always bingo for her to go to. Whenever anything went wrong, or seemed likely to, Mum went out. We were very rarely together, all four of us, as a family. It was as if she would rather be out than in – I knew the feeling, but I didn't have the option. If my dad was there, she would either be at one of her little part-time jobs (cleaning usually), or at a friend's house for a Tupperware party – or at the bingo. It was her favourite get-out option, her way of burying her head in the sand, and it played right into my dad's hands. There was nothing he wanted more than to have an empty house. With no one there to be suspicious at all, he could do whatever he wanted. By this time, I was starting to resent Mum in many ways. Of course, it was only natural that I still craved her attention and affection, but it is also only natural that a dog can only be kicked so many times before it stays down. My love for her was still there, but only in the way that the bonds between mother and child can never be truly broken. She never really acted like a mother, even though I tried my very hardest to be a good daughter. I tried harder than any child should ever have to try, because during all of those years, through all that horrendous abuse, I was doing it for my mum. Every time my father touched me, every time he invaded me, I was doing it not to avoid being hit, not to avoid being called more names – no, I was doing it all for a woman who could barely even look me in the eye.

I wouldn't be human if I hadn't spent a long time – perhaps too long – wondering how much she knew about what was going on. I wondered whether she suspected something about what Dad was doing to me and that was why she pulled herself away, but it didn't make any sense. Why would any mother do that? If she thought her husband was abusing her daughter, why would she not stay and fight? Why would she not accuse him of his terrible crimes? If she felt incapable of doing that, of being assertive and acting in the best interests of her child, she could have protected me in other ways. If she couldn't face up to throwing him out and reporting him to the police, or his employers, why could she just not stay with me? Make sure I was never alone with him, make sure he never had the opportunity to do such awful things to me? None of it made sense – but the overriding thing I hated to remember was that she had never been warm to me. Even before the abuse started, I have no memories of hugs and kisses from her, no memories of cuddling up together reading stories or playing with dollies together. No real love at all.

It breaks my heart to think what I was willing to put up with for a woman who treated me like a stranger. I know there are others who have lived with cold mothers, but, thankfully, their fathers often step up to the plate and give those poor children what they need. What my father gave me, what he forced on me, was no compensation for what my mum withheld. But the saddest thing of all was that when he did those awful things, it was the only affection I was given. When he kissed me, when he stroked my hair, when he held me – all of which he would do before abusing me – that was all I had. That was what I knew of love.

All that had changed was the geography – Dad was still the monster he'd always been.

CHAPTER 12

DANGER

We spent two years in Northern Ireland. For some reason, Dad had thrown out his tape recorder some time before we left Germany. He still read voraciously though – that is one of my strongest memories of him. He drank, he smoked, he treated me appallingly, and he always, always had a cowboy book or a thriller on the go.

Gary and I read a lot from an early age too, mainly the annuals which came out every year – *Jackie*, *Sparky* and *Bunty* for me, *The Broons* for Gary – and I also loved Enid Blyton books. My favourite of all, however, was *Black Beauty*, which I read time and time again. I adored the happy ending.

Mum stopped wearing her short dresses due to constantly getting ulcers on her legs and the resultant scarring. She continued to wear bell-bottoms but replaced her short skirts for maxi dresses. She used to wear tights but changed these for pop socks, which I also wore under my jeans. Fashion and music was changing as always, but parts of my life never altered.

Mum was still buying from Avon when she could but she had to get friends to post things to her as there didn't seem to be any Avon parties in Northern Ireland. The house was covered in Avon tat – Cinderella shoes, bells, candles, small cottage houses and rocking chairs (made from pegs) with smelly pot-pourri cushions. Maybe she was trying to get rid of the smell of stale beer which seemed to permeate everything. I also remember she bought a mood ring. I was fascinated by it and truly believed it showed what you were feeling. The changing colours had different meanings; blue was happy, purple meant moody, and black suggested you were down in the dumps. I would often try it on just to see what my mood was and hoped for the happy colours.

Mum changed her hairstyle shortly after we arrived in Northern Ireland. It was still long but she got herself a curly perm which she liked very much. I remember she bought two large pictures of a crying boy and crying girl, which she put up in the sitting room. She always used to say that the crying girl and I were the same: 'bloody miserable'.

After we had been there about a year, something happened which made me very happy. We got a dog.

One day, Gary came back from school with a little scrap of fur in his arms. I was already home, being on my own personal curfew, but he had been playing football with friends. On the way back, he had found this little puppy shivering by the roadside. She must have only been about three months old, and was a beautiful spaniel and collie crossbreed. That might just be a mongrel to most people, but to me she was the loveliest dog I'd ever seen.

I looked at her in wonder when Gary brought her home.

'Do you think we'll get to keep her?' I asked him.

'We'd better,' he replied, with a steely determination in his voice.

'Can you ask?' I knew he would have a much better chance than me. Luckily, he felt the same way.

'No problem. I've always wanted a dog,' he told me.

He was right. It was no problem, because it was the 'right' child asking for something. Gary played it absolutely perfectly by going to my mum first. He turned his own puppy-dog eyes on her and she was powerless to resist. By the time Dad got in and had settled himself in his chair, drinking, the deal was done. Mum took the puppy through and simply said, 'Harry, we've got a dog.'

'What do we want a dog for?' he asked.

'We just do,' she told him.

'I don't want a dog. I'm doing nothing.'

His retort didn't bother her – I'm sure all that was in her mind was that Gary wanted this puppy, so she'd fight for it if she had to.

'I'm not asking you to do anything, am I? What are you calling it, son?' she asked.

Gary was standing at the doorway in front of me, both of us wondering if we really were going to get to keep it. I whispered to him, 'Betty, I want to call her Betty.' He shrugged. I suspect it was the getting of the dog which mattered to him, not the naming of her.

'She's called Betty,' he told my mum.

'What?' asked my dad, steadily getting more drunk as the conversation went on. 'Bay? That's a fucking stupid name for a dog.' It seemed that the drink was finally having an effect on his faculties. He couldn't pronounce it with his slurred, drunk voice, and no one wanted to contradict him.

'Don't you swear at him,' snapped my mother. 'It's Betty. That's settled.'

I couldn't believe my luck. We were getting to keep the dog, and I had chosen her name. Mum shoved her into Gary's arms as she went to make dinner, and he, in turn, gave her to me. Food was more important than the puppy. I slipped away to my room, closed the door quietly – Dad had said that I wasn't really allowed to shut it – and lay down on my bed with her. I whispered her name over and over, as she licked my face. She was so loving already and I was bursting with happiness that she was going to be part of my life. My dog!

I don't think you can overestimate the comfort any child can get from a pet, but for an abused child it is magnified a hundredfold. As time went on, I'd tell her my worries, I'd cry to her, I would pour all of my frustrations out to her. She was a wonderful outlet for me. Dad always called her Bay, as that was all he could manage when he was drunk. Ironically, that ended up being the only name she responded to – she knew who was in charge too, I suppose.

Towards the end of our two years in Northern Ireland, I would say that Dad became more subdued. I still couldn't count the number of occasions on which he abused me.

While this seems an odd thing to say, given that the whole situation was horrific and degrading, I don't think he got as much enjoyment out of it as he had in Germany. That's why I think he had to take it up a stage.

One night, I came in after taking Betty for a walk. Not only did I now have someone to talk to, but I had actually been given more freedom since we'd got a dog, because Gary got fed up with her very quickly, so I was given the responsibility of exercising her. Mum was at bingo, as usual, and it was starting to get dark, so must have been after 9pm. When I came in, I went straight to the kitchen to get a towel for Betty as it had been raining and I wanted to dry her off. Dad was standing there. I had hoped he would be in the living room, drinking, and I would have been able to get Betty sorted and then sneak off to my room before he knew I was back.

'Come here,' he said, as I tended to the dog.

I pretended I hadn't heard him and soon felt his palm hit my head.

'I know you can hear me, you little bitch,' he said, 'and we both know you'll do as I fucking say. Do you not want to come here?'

I knew it was probably a trick, but I still shook my head and whispered, 'No.'

'Fair enough,' he replied. 'No problem.'

I waited. There was no way that would be the end of it.

'You don't want to come over here, that's fine – that's your choice. We'll do it your way,' he threatened. 'Get up those fucking stairs to my room, now.'

'I don't want to,' I said, although I have no idea where I got the strength from.

'Is that right?' he replied.

'You said it was my choice, Dad,' I reminded him.

'Aye, aye, it is I suppose,' he pondered. 'Fine. You've made your choice.' With those words, he leaned over and put the tap on. 'I'll just drown this little fucking rat, then.' He grabbed Betty as I screamed.

'You will do as I fucking tell you,' he shouted at me, 'and if you don't, you'll suffer the fucking consequences.'

'No, Dad, I don't want to go up there, but please don't hurt Betty!'

'Then say goodbye to this!' he shouted back at me.

There was a lot of screaming going on between both of us, and poor little Betty was barking furiously in the middle of it all while trying to get out of my father's arms, he was squeezing her so tightly. Suddenly, I heard the front door open and Mum shouted, 'What's all this racket?'

She came into the kitchen just as Dad had crossed the room. He threw Betty into the bin as she walked through the door. 'What on earth is going on, Harry? Tracy?'

'False alarm, Valerie,' he said, scooping the dog out of where he had thrown her seconds ago. He handed her to me and I hugged her with all my might. 'Tracy thought she'd lost the dog but the silly wee bugger had just climbed in the bin and was hiding there.'

My Mum just accepted his explanation. She didn't seem to think it odd that a little puppy had climbed into a really high bin and squashed herself in a tiny opening, and she didn't question why there had been so much screaming when my dad had presumably found Betty very quickly. I suppose that was just how she was with everything – she never questioned what he said.

Not long after that, when Dad demanded I go upstairs to his room, I knew I really did have no option. I couldn't lose Betty, and I would just have to face up to what he always did to me. I was getting older and I hated everything about his control over me. Of course, I'd always been terrified and sickened by the abuse, but as I grew up I was starting to question things. Mum seemed a lot better – couldn't we stop? Why couldn't the doctors make her well rather than it all depending on my accepting my dad's violation of me? And, as always, if I was helping, why didn't she love me more? On top of all that, though, was the moral belief that this was just wrong. Dad had said it was our secret and it was a secret that lots of little girls had with their daddies, but these were such horrible things to do that I didn't think other, nicer daddies would put their little girls through it.

By this time, I was quite friendly with Hilary, the girl who lived across the road from us and who sat on the kerb playing on her own quite often. I would never have dared tell her what my dad was doing, but that wasn't just because I was terrified of him; it was also because I suspected the same thing was happening to Hilary. The only 'evidence' I had for this was that she seemed sad a lot of the time and her mum was ill. Maybe Hilary and her dad had the secret too?

Looking out of our window one day, Dad saw me chatting with Hilary as we both sat on the pavement. He knocked on the glass and beckoned for me to come inside. I ran in, more obedient than Betty ever was. 'What are you talking to that girl about?' he demanded.

'Nothing. School. Stuff,' I replied.

'You seem very cosy.' He stared at me. 'You do remember what I've said, Tracy? You can't tell anyone about helping your mum. If you do, she'll get ill again. She could die, Tracy – and it would be your fault. Just remember that next time you're gossiping with your little friend.'

'I'll remember, Dad,' I said and turned to go back outside with Hilary.

'Where the fuck are you pissing off to now, you stupid little bitch?' he snapped. 'Get upstairs. Your mum's not been feeling too well at all – move it.'

The look on his face told me it would be pointless to argue. I walked up to his room with him close behind. He muttered his usual litany against me – *filthy, whore, bitch, dirty, slut.* He pushed me towards the bed and when I made to lie down, he said, 'No, sit up.' I did as I was told and perched on the end of the old divan. He removed his trousers and pants immediately then positioned himself in a sitting position too, up by the headboard. I tried to keep my gaze away from what was between his legs. It was horrible, as always, and I thought that, as he wasn't touching me, he'd want me to masturbate him this time. He leaned over and grabbed me by the wrist. I couldn't help but blurt out, 'I don't want to, Dad, I don't want to touch it,' and tried to pull my hand back.

He smiled. 'Is that right? Well, it's about time you started using your mouth for something other than complaining.' With that, he grabbed me by the hair and pulled me towards his penis. My hair had only recently grown long again. In Germany, he had been so keen on pulling me about by it that it used to come out in clumps. One day, when Mum said she was going to the hairdresser, I asked if I could get mine done too. When I came home with it all chopped off, like a boy, Dad went mad but I was willing to take his shouting as I had removed one of his weapons. He couldn't get a grip on my hair for ages after that, and it was only since we had been in Northern Ireland that it had started to grow long as Mum hadn't found a hairdresser yet. As he dragged me towards him by it, I regretted that I hadn't taken scissors to it myself.

'No!' I shouted when it dawned on me what I was expected to do. I didn't have a full realisation though, as the worst thing I could think of was that he might want me to kiss it – how could I have known what he was really after?

'Go on, you've been fucking desperate for that,' he snarled at me. 'You know exactly what you want, don't you? My little prostitute. That's what you are, my little whore. I bet you'll know just what to do as well, won't you?' He had my hair wrapped around his hand and was holding it close to my scalp so he had a strong grip with which to control my head. He thrust his hips up towards me and manoeuvred my mouth onto him. I kept my lips closed and struggled. 'Open it! Open your fucking mouth!'

I tried to shake my head but could hardly move. I thrashed around, but he was so strong. He pulled my head up to look at him and glowered at me. 'Listen. Your mother will fucking die if you don't do this. Do you even understand? Get your fucking mouth open and get it round that – you'll know what to do when you start.'

He pushed me down again and I did open my mouth. I thought he meant for me to give it a grown-up kiss. I had seen people on TV and films kiss with their lips apart and I told myself that, if I did that, he would let me go, but as soon as my mouth touched his penis, he shoved me towards it with such ferocity that it went straight into my mouth. I tried to jerk back but he wouldn't let me go. I was crying and making a noise like a trapped animal but he kept telling me over and over again how much I liked it, how much I was enjoying it, how much little sluts like me could think of nothing else but this.

The more he pushed me onto him, the harder he seemed to be getting. I could taste horrible things, it was salty and there was something coming out of it. All of a sudden, I could bear it no longer and I gagged. I could feel vomit rising in my throat and there was a light-headedness overwhelming me. The gagging wouldn't stop and as I writhed about he finally threw me off him. 'For fuck's sake, Tracy!' he shouted. 'That's supposed to be nice for me and you've fucking ruined it.' He pulled his pants and trousers on and stormed out of the room.

I lay there crying – as much at his words as his actions. Nice? That was supposed to be nice? I was a child. I couldn't even think how he could come up with the idea to make me do that, as I didn't even know oral sex existed. A light flicked on. He had said that it was meant to be *nice*. Not to help Mum, not to make her better, but to make him feel *nice*.

That wasn't why I was doing this – something changed that night, but I wasn't out of the woods yet.

CHAPTER 13

LUCKY MAN

Maybe it was the location which did it, but Dad seemed to have the luck of the Irish. One day, while I was looking out of my bedroom window after school to see if Hilary was playing on the pavement, I saw an ambulance draw up. It pulled up across the road from our house, but my heart was in my mouth. It could just as easily be for Mum as anyone else. I had assumed she was at bingo when I came in and only Dad was there, but now I wondered.

'Mum? Mum?' I shouted as I jumped down from the seat at the window. Rushing out of my room, I ran straight into Dad. 'What's all the shrieking about?' he asked.

'Mum! Where's Mum?'

'Bingo.'

'Are you sure?' I needed him to confirm things. I needed him to tell me the truth.

'Of course I'm fucking sure – I'm not stupid like you,' he replied. 'What's going on?'

'There's an ambulance out there,' I pointed towards the window, 'and I thought they might be coming in here.'

He walked over to where I had gestured. 'Mmmn,' he said. 'Actually, your mum hasn't been feeling too well, but that's not for her. You need to be very careful, Tracy, it could easily have been here to take her to hospital. You need to make sure you are *always* a good girl.' My heart sank. Although the abuse had been continuing and his strange bathing rituals were as regular as ever, he had never again tried to force me into oral sex. If he was thinking I wasn't being good enough, I could only pray he wouldn't try to force that on me again. 'Think about it,' he said, as he left the room.

I went back to my viewing point just in time to see a stretcher being taken out of Hilary's house. I could vaguely see a woman's face and knew it was her mum, not mine. I had long held suspicions that Hilary was abused too, but these thoughts were purely down to her being sad and a loner. When I had discovered some time ago that her mum didn't keep well either – these illnesses were never really specified in my youth when children were expected to be seen and not heard – then it all fell into place for me. If her mum was ill, if she was sad, then she would have a secret with her dad.

With my own father's words ringing in my ears, I could only think one thing. Hilary hadn't been good. She hadn't been good *enough* and now her mum was being taken into hospital. I wondered what Hilary had refused to do? Had her daddy tried to get her to do the horrible thing with her mouth as well?

I didn't see Hilary that day – or for the rest of the week. About ten days after I had seen the ambulance pull up in our street, I came home one half-day to the sight of a line of hearses outside her front door. Running inside, I could hardly bear to watch them from the window but I caught a glimpse of Hilary walking beside her father. She was pale and tiny; it was like looking at myself, I thought.

My dad used to appear beside me as if he had supernatural powers. Maybe I was often in a world of my own or maybe he just liked to catch me unawares, but this was one of those times. As I stood with tears falling from my eyes, thinking of Hilary's loss and of what it would mean for me if my own mum died, he was there with an arm around my shoulders.

'Sad, isn't it?' he said. 'So sad when a little girl's mummy dies. Hilary will be all on her own now, I guess – I hope her dad doesn't mind looking after her.'

'Why would he mind?' I asked.

'Well, if Hilary hasn't been a good girl, if it's her fault that her mum died, then I suppose her dad would be within his rights to be very angry.'

'Was it Hilary's fault?' I asked quietly.

'I would think so,' he confirmed. 'I hope it's making you think, Tracy. It's a terrible thing when a daughter doesn't love her mum enough. Can you imagine how that poor woman must have felt on her deathbed knowing it was her own child who put her there?'

'Will ... will that happen to my mum?' I stammered.

'I don't know.' He shook his head. 'I really don't know.

120

We can only hope that you'll learn a lesson from this and be a very, very good girl from now on. That would be a terrible thing to have on your conscience for the rest of your life.'

It was a lucky day for my father when Hilary's mum died – and he would make the most of it. Things had been changing slightly in that I was being much more vocal about my opposition to the abuse. There had been occasions when I had actually run away from him and locked myself in the upstairs bathroom until Mum or Gary came home, in order to thwart his intentions. That wasn't easy. He'd stand outside, banging on the door, shouting and swearing, calling me all the names he could think of and threatening to batter me senseless when he finally did get his hands on me, but all I would think of at those times was that I was at least delaying what he wanted to do, and every minute without it happening was a minute I savoured.

There had also been times when he had tried to drag me into his bedroom by my hair, and I had physically fought him off. I have plenty of physical mementoes of those days and nights. He liked to hit my back and the back of my head. He enjoyed kicking and punching me in the kidneys, where it was hidden but a lot of pain could be inflicted. He had lots of favourite places. To this day, I have a rib always out of place because of what he did – whenever I've been X-rayed, doctors have said I must have had it cracked when it was young, but I have always been evasive about how it actually happened.

Sometimes I would be able to keep him off until someone

came back, or, a couple of times, as had happened the time he had tried to force me to give him oral sex, he would rant at me and say that I had 'spoiled' things. I didn't always win. There were times when he caught me, dragged me to his room, and abused me in anger, which was always even more painful than usual. He was letting his true side show more and more often; there simply wasn't always the pretence that it was for Mum, or that we were doing this for a greater good. It was becoming more and more clear to me that he enjoyed this and when his perfect scenario wasn't played out, he would be furious.

The fact that I was making it clear I didn't want this was a big difference. Even if it did help Mum – and I wasn't always sure about that, although the death of Hilary's mother had blurred the lines again – I was more aware of sex, and realised that was exactly the sort of 'relationship' my father and I had. And that was wrong. He must have felt so powerful that he could ignore my pleas and screams and still get me to indulge his perversions. He was forcing me every time. Of course, he had always forced me in that it was always abuse, but when I was much younger I was more naive and simply accepted his reasons even when it hurt and made me feel awful. Now, I could shout out against it and he could still make sure it happened; I think that was an enormous power trip for him.

Mum seemed oblivious. She hadn't been ill for a while but, apart from the death of Hilary's mother, Dad wasn't using that excuse very much to control me. She had a little job doing a few hours cleaning each week – he liked that because it got her out of the house even more. One night, just after she left, he told me to get my arse upstairs. I refused and he threatened me, as usual. There was nothing new in the threats, nothing new in the words he used or the punishments he shouted about, but I just couldn't bear the thought of him pawing me that night. I ran upstairs to the bathroom, as I'd done many times before, and he chased me. Just before I got the door closed, he reached in, grabbing me by my jumper. I had a blouse on underneath and I heard them both rip as the material was snatched. I threw all of my weight against the door and slammed it in his face. He ranted and raved at the locked door, but eventually gave up. I decided I had to get out – I dragged the laundry basket over to the bathroom window and stood on it. I could climb out and get away. As I climbed up, I saw the fabric of my jumper and blouse flapping about. Wriggling out of them, I popped them in the laundry basket and rescued a top I'd placed there the day before.

I climbed up, clambered out of the window and dropped onto the low roof below. It was then just another jump to freedom. I didn't do much. I wandered around the camp for a bit, then realised I had to get home. It was cold, I had no money, no friends, and nowhere to go.

When I got home, he was sitting on the sofa with Mum, the ripped clothes from the laundry basket in his hands. 'What do you have to say for yourself?' she asked me. Before I could speak, he interrupted. 'I told you, Valerie – she wanted to go out, I said she couldn't, she had a temper tantrum, and even ruined her good clothes.'

'I just don't know what to do with you,' Mum sighed.

He did.

He got off that sofa and battered me right in front of my mother, who sat there stony-faced, as unemotional as if she was drinking a cup of tea.

This is the woman I was trying to save.

I believe that event made Dad realise I was slipping out of his control. I was getting older, understanding more, and questioning things. He could still force me, he always could, but never again would I quietly comply with his abuse of me.

He needed to up his game; he needed to go to the next level.

He needed to rape me.

When awful things happen in life, you don't always remember every detail. I've had to put together so many little parts of that awful night, because it is the *act* itself which is imprinted on my memory and will be for the rest of my life. From the bits of the jigsaw I have collated, I do know that Mum was, of course, at bingo that night. I know that it was just after Christmas, because I had a new *Jackie* annual. I know that it was a normal day – and one of the most awful ones of my life.

Dad hadn't actually been doing anything to me for a while, certainly since well before Christmas, and I think he may have been lulling me into a false sense of security, or building up to it. It may have been that he was in two minds about whether he was going to take his abuse to the next, abominable level and, certainly, I knew from his reactions during some previous encounters that he was getting more and more angry about me continually saying that I didn't want to do these things.

Maybe he was having a crisis of conscience. I hope so, but doubt it. Even if that was the case, he must have managed to convince himself that it was fine after all, that his own personal depraved sexual needs came before anything else, as always.

When I got home from school, Mum was already making dinner, a sure sign that she was planning to go out. Gary wasn't there as it was his night for Scouts, and Mum said she'd pick him up on her way home from bingo. As soon as the three of us had eaten, Dad snapped at me to go and get a bath. It was barely five o'clock but when I questioned this, he said I was mucky from playing and school. This was the first thing which should have rung an alarm bell – when I hadn't been abused by him, it was up to me to decide when I bathed. The baths after abuse were part of his ritual and he wasn't interested at any other time as to when I washed. Now I was getting older, I was much more aware of personal hygiene and more able to take care of myself – I made sure I washed when Mum was there and, although I was never dressed very well, I was a lot better than in those early days when I smelled and was always called names.

I did as I was told and when I came down Mum was putting her coat on. Although it was still early, she liked to get a particular seat at bingo so tended to meet her friends well before it started. Dad told me to get back to my room and have an early night – I could read for a while, but he'd come up to tell me to put my light out.

'It's fine,' I told him, nervously, not wanting him in my room at all. 'I'll just read for five minutes.' I would rather do that and then pretend to sleep than risk him coming in to me.

'Disobeying me again,' he said, pointedly directing the comment to my mother. 'Why are you such a bad girl, Tracy? As I've said, *I'll* tell you when to put the light out.'

I trotted off to my room and resigned myself to a horrific night – I had no idea just how bad it was going to be. When he came into my room and climbed on top of me, I thought it would be like any other night, but there was something about his attitude, the look in his eye, which panicked me, and I tried to push him off my body.

He said nothing, just forced himself on top of me a little more strongly before starting to touch me all over. He pushed my nightdress up and his horrible nicotine-stained fingers found their way inside my pants. He pulled those off and started hurting me so badly; he was rougher than I could ever remember. His fingers were going so much further than they ever had before; I didn't think I could stand it. Dad was panting and getting out of breath. I hoped it would be over soon.

He took off everything I was wearing and removed all of his clothes, which worried me as I had hoped that the rough touching would have finished things quickly. If he was removing his things, it meant he was planning to be here for a while. He lay on his side and I lay on my back. The

126

stench of him was horrible. I didn't smell any drink on him, but he had been given Brut aftershave for Christmas by my mum and it wasn't enough to keep the smell of sweat away, so there was a stink of body odour mingled in with it which made me want to gag.

As he lay there beside me, he stroked my hair and said that I was his 'little whore'. I tried to imagine I was somewhere else and this wasn't happening, but the smell and his words kept pulling me back. I told him I didn't want to do this but he kept saying Mum would get ill and it would be my fault. She had been saying she was feeling bad that week and that she didn't want it all to start again, so when he told me to lie there and she would get better, I was torn.

He stopped touching me for a few minutes while he kept up his chant of sexual insults, and continued to stroke me and say that I loved all of this – and then he began to shove his fingers inside me again. As soon as he started again, I knew this would be worse than any other time. It was intrusive. It was hideous. I started gagging again but he ignored me and climbed on top. 'You're Daddy's girl,' he said, 'you're my little darling.' I could feel that he was hard and I could feel that he was pushing his penis into me, but this was going beyond anything he'd done in the past.

Then he entered me.

I thought the pain was going to split me into little pieces.

I didn't think I could cope with that, didn't think I could survive it. I know now that you can survive almost anything. All of the time he was thrusting at me, he was saying that I was a whore, a bitch, his whore, his bitch.

It seemed to take forever.

When he finished and got off me, I think I was in shock. I couldn't move, not just because of the pain, but because I knew that this was the worst thing of all – and that if he had done it once, he'd do it again. He never went back, he always upped things a level. I shouldn't have worried about moving because he told me to stay still anyway and then pulled his clothes on before leaving the room.

I was shaking but not crying until he returned with a bottle-green plastic basin filled with hot water, a bar of soap and a washing flannel.

He washed me this time – the ritual had changed. As he rubbed the soap over me and rinsed it off with the flannel, he kept calling me his favourite names. *Little prostitute, little prostitute, my little prostitute*, he muttered constantly as he washed between my legs. I was feeling sick and I was hurting. I could feel where bruises would appear over the next few hours.

Dad told me that everything would be all right – but I couldn't see how. Then I realised he wasn't referring to me or how I was feeling, he wasn't actually concerned about the child he had just raped. He meant that his lies and illusions about my mum would be realised. 'You'll see,' he promised, 'Mum will be fine now.' He was taking a huge risk with that as this was the first time he had really abused me *before* she was obviously ill.

After he had completed the ritual, his tone changed again. 'You're filthy,' he said. 'Get out of that fucking bed and have a bath.' Still in shock, I staggered to the bathroom while he remained in the bedroom. He was changing the bed linen – I never saw the sheets as he removed them, but there must have been blood, which was why he washed me to begin with that night. Once I had run the bath and got in, he came into the bathroom and sat on the seat as he usually did. He stared at me for twenty minutes and I was in such a state that I didn't even move, nor did I ask if I could get out until he finally left the room and I came to my senses.

I went back to my bedroom and put on baggy pyjamas. I could hear him doing some washing in the kitchen and vaguely wondered what lie he would tell my mum to cover his tracks about why there was wet bedding and clothing lying around. I didn't even bother to think about whether she would question him – I knew she accepted every word which came out of his mouth.

I climbed into my bed and lay in the darkness with my eyes wide open for hours. I heard the other sounds of the house go on as normal as Gary and my mum came back, and I existed in my own little world. Alone as always. Not the lucky one.

CHAPTER 14

NORMAL

I continued to fear every glance my father threw in my direction as the outside world around me was becoming more and more dangerous. As hundreds of people were imprisoned without trial, protests increased in number and ferocity. The one which took place in Derry on 30 January 1972 would change everything and become known the world over as Bloody Sunday.

The march had been organised by the Northern Ireland Civil Rights Association to protest against internment and, although it had been banned by the province's Stormont government, later news footage would show there was a happy, upbeat atmosphere, with lots of families among the thousands who had attended. There was singing, and a real sense of camaraderie. There were plans for the ten thousand or so to walk from the Creggan Estate to Guildhall Square in the centre of the city, where a rally would be held. Members of the Paratroop Regiment had sealed off the Square to prevent this, so a different route was decided at the last minute, but some protestors stayed behind to confront the soldiers – they responded with rubber bullets, CS gas and a water cannon. The gas forced many into an area called Bogside and it was there that the soldiers opened fire, killing thirteen people in a space of twenty-five minutes.

For all of us in British Army accommodation, it meant that a match had finally been thrown into the tinderbox in which we lived. Within a couple of months, Stormont would be suspended, and the number of deaths would increase almost tenfold. A quick decision was made – all families were to be moved out as quickly as possible.

The day after Bloody Sunday, Mum was waiting for me after school. 'Get your stuff sorted,' she snapped. 'We're moving and there's no time to waste.' I didn't have much to organise or pack, but I still needed to know why it all had to be done in such a rush. 'Don't ask so many questions,' she answered. 'We've got a week to get out of this hellhole – if we're lucky enough to make it in one piece.' I heard from people at school the next day that they'd all been given the same message. We had to get out, and we had to get out quickly. My only concern was Betty and whether we could take her with us. My Dad said 'not bloody likely', but luckily someone who worked in one of the local shops had always had a soft spot for her and was happy to give her a home. I'd miss her terribly but at least I knew she was safe and away from the kicks my dad sent her way all too regularly.

No one knew exactly what would happen as a result of

the Bloody Sunday murders, but there was no doubt in anyone's mind that there would be repercussions, with everyone associated with the British Army in the firing line.

While Mum seemed harassed – probably because she carried the burden of getting accommodation moves organised, and I guess there was always the chance the extra stress could bring on her illness again – Dad was delighted. He was a different character in Northern Ireland and I sensed that a move elsewhere would allow him to reinvent himself yet again.

Throughout that week, the pressure to move quickly intensified; all the families on the first evacuation out to other bases were anxious, and the aftermath of Bloody Sunday meant we were just waiting to see what atrocity would happen next. As I've been writing this book, so many decades after the events, the Inquiry into that day has finally concluded. The very fact that it has been in the news yet again has taken me back to those days. In the midst of such a terrible mark on British history, I've had to face up to what was happening to one little girl. While the world looked on in horror at the atrocities in Northern Ireland, I was living out my own nightmare – and, sadly, I wouldn't be the only child doing so.

We got back to Germany quickly, where I kept myself to myself for a while, not speaking to people apart from when I needed to at school, and not really developing any proper friendships. This was quite odd for an Army kid. Mum always managed to establish good, if superficial, friendships within a few weeks of moving to a new posting. She never complained about moving to other postings or about leaving friends behind. Women knew what they needed to do if they were Army wives. There wasn't time to waste as you never knew when you might be moving on, and they also never knew when they might need someone, so they all built up support networks pretty quickly. Throughout the whole Army experience, she could pick up friends quickly and then drop them when she moved on. There were no tears on leaving, no promises to write or stay in touch, and the days of Facebook and email were decades away, so when families moved on, that was it. My brother was similar to her. He got a new gang very quickly each time we moved somewhere else. I don't think I was an unfriendly child, but I still bore the psychological scars of when I had been called names. I was no longer smelly and unkempt, but I was still an outsider. What had been done to me made sure of that. How could I trust anyone? How could I believe anyone's story? I of all people knew just how many lies were perpetuated by families, and just how different private lives could be to the ones presented for public consumption.

Throughout my time in Singapore and Germany, then on to Northern Ireland, I had largely kept a distance from everyone. However, when we returned to Rinteln, I found there were girls around who I had known the first time, so I didn't have to start from scratch. It was easier for me to develop the slim threads of friendship from my younger days and try to make them stronger. I hadn't managed to acquire my mum's and Gary's ability to make friends quickly and not bother about the prospect of never seeing them again, but I was more willing to take a chance this time. As an Army child, you do learn to avoid getting too emotionally attached and to hold a part of yourself back. As an abused child, I was actually quite good at this. I could be whatever I needed to be for the company I was in as I was used to living a lie anyway.

When we'd first left Rinteln for Northern Ireland, we didn't know we would be back one day – in fact, Hong Kong had been on the cards, so we had broken all ties. With Singapore and Northern Ireland, we had been given six months' notice in advance, but it was much quicker after Bloody Sunday. Some families spoke of sometimes having no warning at all, and of having to drag out their MFO boxes for a move the next day, so there was a sense of never really settling into anything, to school, friendships, or even pets. If you accumulated personal belongings, you often had to leave them behind. Emotional ties fitted into that category as well.

It wasn't a traumatic way of living if you didn't know any different. In some ways, that was what I felt about the abuse for a while too. My dad had been so clever about how he had manipulated me that I had accepted this was just what some daddies did with their daughters. In fact, as far as I knew, maybe *all* daddies did this with all little girls. Certainly, if their mums were ill, this was a way for good girls to help make them better, and who wouldn't see that as a price worth paying? Although I hated the abuse, and although I was beginning to realise it was wrong, my father was

134

trying very hard to normalise it over all those years, so it was a way of living that was normal for me.

Just as I spent my days waiting for signs of whether my dad was getting ready to rape me again, I watched for symptoms of Mum's illness. I remember how she used paraffin cream to cover the ulcers which would develop. When I saw her rubbing paraffin in or having a paraffin bath, I started to worry. Dad's luck held for a while after raping me for the first time and she stayed out of hospital until about six months after we moved back to Germany.

The abuse and rape continued and, unsurprisingly, there were physical consequences. It was more surprising there hadn't been anything requiring medical attention earlier. One morning, quite soon after we returned to Rinteln, I woke up feeling awful. It was hard to put my finger on anything specific and I actually suspect my body was just crying out against all that was being inflicted upon it.

Mum had to get the doctor in not long after we returned to Germany. I was aching all over and had really bad stomach cramps. I was having breathing problems and panic attacks. My body was just screaming that something was wrong and someone needed to listen. My parents stood just inside the bedroom door when the doctor arrived and stayed there throughout the visit. He examined my stomach, throat and ears in quite a cursory way and decided it was a tummy bug. All through the examination, Dad had been chatting away, telling the man about Mum's illness and how she had been recently – trying to distract him, I guess. He had been doing this since the doctor arrived as I had heard them discussing the big, black rubber bullet displayed on our wall – every soldier had been given one of these macabre mementoes when they left Northern Ireland after their tour. Would I have said anything to the doctor if I had been left alone with him? I don't know. Maybe not, but I didn't have the opportunity. Would he have had a more thorough look at me and asked more about my symptoms? He wouldn't have had to look far, and if he had bothered to look underneath my pyjamas he would have seen the enormous damage which had been inflicted on my body.

As the doctor got up to leave, I made one attempt at making him see there was something terribly wrong. 'I'm smelly, I smell, I smell all over, I smell.'

It was as if I could see the colour drain from my dad's face. My Mum said, 'What's she saying, Harry? What's she saying?'

I tried again. 'I smell. I smell so bad.'

'What do you mean?' the doctor asked. He looked totally bemused but my dad regained his composure very quickly. He walked over to the bed and took my hand. 'I know exactly what she means,' he said. He squeezed my hand tighter and dug his nails into me. 'It's all that Avon stuff Valerie puts in here.' He waved his free hand around my room at the various soaps and pomanders Mum had filled the room with. They were lined up along the pelmet and window ledges. They were the only personal things she ever gave me. 'That's what she means by smelly – she's feeling ill with this tummy bug and all she can sniff is this lavender muck. I'll get it all dumped, leave it to me.'

The doctor seemed to accept that without question although it seemed to make very little sense. He gave me Dioralyte and left. As soon as he closed the door on the doctor, Dad came back in with a rubbish bag and swept all my Avon things away. They were the only nice things I had. To this day, I hate the smell of lavender – I liked it then, but now it just reminds me of that dark time. Even that tiny bit of normal was to be taken away from me.

That was a wake-up call for me. I was getting nowhere being a good girl – it was time for me to try a different approach. I think this happens with a lot of abused children. They're told to be good, they're told to behave, they're told to keep in line – and when they do, they're beaten and raped and betrayed. So, if that's what happens when they're good, why not be bad?

After the incident when the doctor had been called out, I decided it was time to try a little more resistance. What I wanted was for the abuse to stop – that simply wasn't happening. Dad ignored me when I said no and he pinned me down when I struggled. The one way I was able to disobey him was by making friends at school. He had no idea what went on there. I also started taking my time coming home each day, and that worked out quite well as it was during the daytime that Mum was more likely to be there and she preferred it if I stayed out longer as it meant I wasn't around her. The first few times I did come home late, she – without knowing it – really helped me by arguing my side against Dad and claiming it was 'only normal' for girls my age to want to be with their friends.

As a result, since we'd returned to Rinteln, I had got quite chummy with a few older girls. They gave me an insight into what other lives were like and I started to become more aware of fashion and superficial things. I made it known (to my parents, brother and peers) that my taste in music had changed. I started to listen to hard rock and wrote the names of the bands on my school jotters. This was a conscious decision for me – I had noticed that the bad girls seemed to like the same music as boys and I thought it would get me some attention. It was a time of change – clothes, as always, determined which 'gang' you were associated with. The good girls wore ponchos, trouser suits and culottes, while the bad ones were into Doc Martens, hot pants, platform shoes, skinners, bomber jackets and the dreaded tartan shirts and trousers. I had a poncho which I hated – it was hand-knitted and multi-coloured. I deliberately put a hole in it and told Mum I had torn it on a fence. It definitely didn't fit in with the image I was trying to cultivate. I had bottle-green hot pants which I used to wear with platform shoes. The soles were two inches thick and had a palm tree carved on the side. The hairstyle of the time was flicked out in Farrah Fawcett style, which I attempted – unsuccessfully.

Holly Barton was a captain's daughter from a really well-respected family. She was always friendly towards me and we often hung out together. Holly was a little bit wayward, and I liked her because of this. It was nothing too bad – she'd play chap door run, and break windows on abandoned buildings. I hadn't fully decided to become a bad girl yet, but Holly would help me on my way. I actually wanted to fit in with the nice girls at that stage, but Holly and another girl called Glenda Miller would show me that you could have a good time being naughty. The strange thing was, I had known these girls a bit before we left for Northern Ireland, and they hadn't been particularly friendly then, but when I came back they seemed pleased to see me. Maybe kids just grow up very quickly at that stage, or maybe I had changed a lot; whatever the reason, everyone appeared very different. I did meet some nice kids when we got back to Germany, but my behaviour put the good ones off. We all hung round the NAAFI a lot and I bought a few records there with any money I did have – my first one was the Beatles – and some people swapped them too.

One Saturday, I made the most of my mum being at home again and went into town with Holly and Glenda. I'd never been in a 'gang' before and was really excited – however, I had no idea until we went into the German hypermarket that the other girls were planning to shoplift. They hadn't discussed it on the way there, but it seemed so natural to them I could only assume they did this regularly. It turned out I was a natural too. I loved make-up but wasn't allowed it – without a hint of irony, my dad said it would make me look like a tart and that boys would be sniffing around. When Holly and Glenda started nicking sweets, I headed for the cosmetics counter and filled my pockets with lipsticks and eye shadows. It was all the German equivalent of Miners or Rimmel. Holly and Glenda gave me some of what they had stolen too, sweetie bracelets and dark chocolate, which was much more expensive in those days.

I felt quite pleased with myself as we made our way home. It had been a real bonding experience and I had shown the other girls that, despite being younger, I could do what I needed to do to be part of their gang. They were pleased with me, and with the make-up loot I shared with them, and I was on a high. I wasn't really too bothered about getting caught as I thought that getting out of the shop without someone noticing would be the main thing, but once Holly and Glenda had gone home, I did start to think about where I could hide my stash. I didn't have much money to spend, so I knew Mum or Dad would be suspicious if they found anything. Just outside my bedroom window was a huge tree; when I got back, I put all the make-up and sweets in a plastic bag, tied the handles and hung it on a branch. I clearly wasn't destined to become a criminal mastermind because Mum saw it waving about out there the moment she came into my room. 'Tracy? There's something in that bag hanging on the tree out there,' she commented.

'I don't think so,' I tried to say calmly. 'Bags are always getting caught in the wind.'

'No – there's something in there. It looks heavy,' she said.

She opened the window and reached out – it wasn't hard to grab the bag, after all, a ten-year-old had put it there. Mum stood, holding on to it after she'd looked inside, with her face all twisted up in that special 'mum' look that mixes disappointment with anger.

'Where is this all from?'

'Don't know.'

'Where were you today?'

'Town.'

'Who were you with?'

'Can't remember.'

It was the sort of conversation children have been having with parents for years – a list of questions from her, followed by me giving out as little information as possible. She held the trump card though.

'Tracy, do you remember what I've said to you and Gary about stealing?'

'I didn't steal anything!' I lied.

'Well, that's fine then – you won't be bothered about me calling the police and asking them to get to the bottom of it.'

With that, she flounced out of the room with the bag in her hand and a commitment to her version of tough love. Mum kept to her word and the police arrived that evening. I denied it all for a little while and then Dad came in. He asked the policemen if they would mind him having a quick chat with me in private. He took me out of the living room, and asked if I had taken it. I admitted I had, hoping he would say he would sort it all out – surely he owed me something? – but he seemed completely nonplussed by having police in the house, and went straight through to tell them he had got to the bottom of it.

I was told I had to take the stuff back to the shop and one of the police officers said they would be putting this on record and watching for me. I had no idea if that was true, but as soon as they left my mum started ranting and raving.

'You'd better get her sorted out!' she screamed at Dad. 'I'm sick of her bad behaviour.'

The thing was, I had never stolen before and the only 'evidence' she had of my so-called bad behaviour was all the lies Dad told her.

'What do you mean?' I asked. 'What have I ever done wrong?'

'Your father's told me all about it.'

'I've done nothing, I'm a good girl,' I protested.

'Good girls don't lie and steal,' she retorted, then sighed. 'Oh, I'm too ill to put up with this. You deal with her, Harry. I'm so cross with that girl, I need to get out of here.'

Off she went to the bingo while my father smirked on the sofa.

As soon as she was out of the door, I knew what would happen. And it did. He was so angry at me, which made him even rougher than usual. Afterwards, he said, 'You were told, Tracy – you know the rules. When you play up, your mother gets ill, and now the fucking police are involved. How much worse do you think that makes her? You need to fucking behave.'

I didn't know what else to do. I let him hurt me. I let him rape me. What else did he want? I didn't know at that stage it was all about power and controlling me. There wasn't anything I could do apart from let him rule my life. 'You told Mum I was doing bad things but I'm a good girl, aren't I?'

He thought about it for a moment. 'You're my good girl, but you're her bad girl. Do you want her to love you?'

'Yes. Yes, I do.'

'Then you do what I tell you. You do everything I tell you. I'll show you how to make her love you.' Even as I lay there, bleeding and in agony, that's all I could think of.

Throughout the following week, Mum was really unwell. Dad said it was because she was terribly upset about the shame I had brought on her, which was worsened when he took me back to the supermarket to return the stolen goods. The manager was actually really good about it and said I had done well by being honest, but Dad made a big fuss when we got back and said to Mum that I had shown us all up. A few days later, her legs needed to be strapped up with the pain and she had bleeding, blistering mouth ulcers, which meant she could barely eat. I thought it was my fault – and Dad made the most of it. She wasn't going out, so he had to abuse me in my own bed, usually in the middle of the night. I never knew when he would be there; I could never settle or relax. These restrictions also meant he couldn't engage in the washing ritual as Mum would notice a bath being run in the middle of the night, so he was angry all the time.

She was taken into hospital one weekend for a few days and he abused me solidly throughout that period. Gary was at football practice, at friends, playing outside and my dad kept me away from my friends, using the excuse to Gary that they were a bad influence and that he had to keep an eye on me. By the time Mum got back, I felt physically, emotionally and mentally drained – perhaps he felt a little bit guilty, if he was capable of that, because I think he must have had a word with her. Something certainly happened, because the Saturday after she got home, she suggested we went on a day out.

I couldn't believe it. We started off by going to the cinema then went to the shops. She bought me a lovely pink jumpsuit (it seemed lovely in 1973!), denim culottes, Wrangler jeans and Doc Marten boots, so many of the things I'd dreamed of. I had decided how I wanted to look, and – apart from the pink jumpsuit – it was a very boyish, hard look, which would be in line with my behaviour. It was our first and last girly day out. My birthday was only a few weeks away and I asked whether all of these things were my presents, but she said they were extra. We were laden with shopping, we went for a cream bun in a café – we appeared to all the world like a normal mum and daughter. At one point, I reached for her hand, but that was a step too far for her and she snatched it away. She still held Gary's hand when they were out, and he was a teenager. My father had played it very well. He must have told her I was going off the rails, so she should take me out and see if it made a difference. I didn't think that at the time though; I just believed that being a good girl for him had finally paid off.

I was disproportionately grateful to her for doing what so many mums did as a matter of course. That gratitude extended to my dad as well, for I had no doubt he had made this happen. I revelled in the normality of it – and it lasted for a while.

For a couple of weeks, Mum was much better with me. She wasn't loving but she would do things she'd never done before, such as sit beside me on the sofa while I did my reading – I would deliberately get things wrong so she would help. Usually she only sat there with Gary, hugging him, while I was told to go and do my homework at the table. When it stopped and she reverted back to type, I did the only thing I could think of – I tried to get attention.

In Germany, the camp was more laid-back than it had been in Northern Ireland, and more than it had been when we were there before. It was a fifteen-minute walk from town and more like a housing scheme for Englishers, as we were known (despite being Scottish!). There was a building site nearby where they were just putting windows into new houses and that's where I headed, feeling very hard in my DMs and Wranglers. The police drove by regularly and I made sure I was throwing rocks at the glass just as they went by on one of their circuits. There was no point doing it if I didn't get caught. It was a conscious decision when I went out that day to do something that would get me attention. I was taken back home in the car to Mum. When Dad came home, her only words were, 'She's been at it again.'

As usual, Mum left the house as soon as she had handed over responsibility to him and, as usual, I was punished by him forcing himself upon me. He was in a set pattern. He'd always wash me. It didn't hurt or bruise so much by then, so maybe I was getting used to it. It certainly felt as if he was pushing deeper each time. I was eleven years old by this time and it's probably only now, as a mother and grandmother, that I see the true horror of what was going on – what does it take for an eleven-year-old child to be glad that her body is getting more used to her father raping her because it doesn't hurt quite so much any more? I can see there were many times when he wasn't angry, when he actually treated me like a lover, caressing me, stroking my hair. He had crossed another line and seemed to see me as a substitute wife. My father now thought this was all perfectly normal, I think. He would ask if I was enjoying myself, if it had been good for me, if I liked the way he touched me. He obviously wanted me to say 'yes' because that would normalise it even more for him. I'd ask, 'Why? Why do you want me to say "yes"? You know I don't want this, Dad.' He told me it should make me feel happy inside. That was the last thing it did, but by now he had broken me.

This was my life, this was my normality.

CHAPTER 15

A MAN WITH FRIENDS

Billy Stoppard was one of my dad's drinking buddies. I don't know how much deeper that link went – but I was about to find out part of it. He was a big man, physically imposing and in a different regiment to my father, although he was a proper soldier not an impostor like Dad.

One day I came back from school and my parents were sitting in the living room chatting to another couple. It was Billy and his wife, Chrissie. Mum knew Chrissie from bingo and that's what they were chatting about. I heard Billy say, 'Fancy going out tonight?' and Chrissie replied by asking him where he was taking her. He laughed and said, 'No, I'm working – why don't you have a night out with Valerie at the bingo?'

Chrissie said she had no one to look after their three kids, who were only little and not at school yet. Billy looked at my dad and smirked. 'That's a shame, love – isn't it, Harry?' He paused. 'Here, Harry – don't suppose you've got any ideas, have you?'

My dad smiled too. 'Well, Tracy's a big girl now, isn't she? Would you like her?'

'I think that would be absolutely perfect,' retorted Billy. 'What do you think, Chrissie?'

I was quiet and tall for my age. I looked like the sort of kid who could take on responsibility, so Chrissie had no reason to worry. 'It's only for a couple of hours I suppose,' she said. 'Is that all right with you, Valerie? The kids will be sleeping anyway.' My mum shrugged, probably wondering why anybody would want to spend time with me if they didn't have to, and Dad sealed the deal. 'Sounds good to me,' he said to Billy. 'She could do with a bit of pocket money, so make sure you pay her.'

'For her services!' Billy laughed.

I wasn't sure about it but I was keen to make some money and Dad said I would get ten Deutschmarks for my trouble. There was a school skiing trip coming up which I really wanted to go on and Dad had said if I could save the money up by myself, I could go. This had seemed like quite a concession from him. It had only been a couple of days before, and I now see he was softening me up for Billy's approach. By planting the seed in my mind that if I could get the money I could go on the trip, he knew I would see the babysitting as a means to an end.

Later that night, he said he would walk me round to Billy and Chrissie's while Mum got ready for bingo. 'Now, you must be a good girl for him, OK?' he warned me as we approached their house. 'You be really, really good.'

I didn't pay attention to Dad; I was just glad to get the

night away from him. Chrissie put the kids in bed before she left and said she'd give me my money when she came back from bingo ('and a wee bit extra if I'm lucky tonight!'), then left. After about an hour, the door opened and Billy came in.

'I thought you were working tonight, Mr Stoppard,' I said.

'Did you now?' he replied. 'Well, you're in luck because I managed to get back to you so much quicker than we expected.' He was really sleazy and I just wanted to get out. Their house had a different layout from ours so I would have had to follow him through to the kitchen from the sitting room to get my money. Something told me I shouldn't do this, so I grabbed my coat and headed for the door. He shouted through, 'Where are you off to? I haven't given you your money yet!' I told him not to bother, that he could pass it on to my dad next time he saw him, but he followed me through and said, 'I insist.'

He pinned me against the front door and started rubbing my shoulders, as if giving me a massage. I said, 'I have to go straight home, I have to go straight home,' but it made no difference.

'You need paying, don't you? That's what your dad said – he told me you like to get paid.'

He kept rubbing my shoulders but his hands were moving further and further down my body. He stopped for a moment and held ten Deutschmarks out in front of me. 'There you go – you'll have to give me a cuddle for it though.'

I looked at the floor and muttered that I wanted to leave.

'Didn't your dad tell you to be good for me?' he said. 'He told me you were such a good girl.'

The penny dropped.

The phrase was the one my dad always used – and I suddenly remembered what he had said when he left me at Billy and Chrissie's front door. *Be good for him.* Billy wasn't meant to be there that night, so why had Dad said that? The only explanation was that he knew Billy would be there. This was all a set-up. My dad had sent me there to be abused.

Billy Stoppard put his arms around me and gave me a cuddle. He slipped the ten Deutschmarks into my pocket, taking too long to do it, then slapped my backside and told me he looked forward to seeing me again.

I ran home as fast as my legs could carry me, not recognising the irony that I was hurrying from one abuser to another. As soon as I went in, Dad said, 'What did you get?' I showed him the ten Deutschmarks. 'So, you were good for him?' he asked. I nodded and put the money in my piggy bank.

The following week, he asked me in front of Mum if I wanted to babysit for Billy and Chrissie's kids again. My mum interrupted before I had a chance to answer. 'Of course she does – gets her out of the house and she'll get paid.' That was it; that was it all settled. Again, he wasn't there when I got to their house but Chrissie said he might be home before her. It was only about ten minutes after she left that he appeared, stinking of booze. I tried to get past him but he stood in front of me. 'You can't go yet – what about your money?'

'I've only been here a little while, I don't mind,' I told him.

He pulled me towards him and started to run his hands all over me as I told him to stop. I pushed him away as much as I could and said 'no' over and over again. 'I'll tell your dad you weren't a good girl,' he said. 'He'll have to punish you, he'll have to make you understand who your friends are.'

'Let me go!' I screamed, managing to get the door open.

'You little bitch!' he said. As I ran out the door he threw a packet of dates at me – 'Take these! You're getting nothing else!'

I cried all the way home. When I got in, Dad asked me how much I'd earned. When I showed him the dates and said there was no money, he asked me whether Chrissie had come home early. It was clear he knew exactly what was going on as he could only think that the reason I hadn't been paid by Billy was that he hadn't got what he wanted because his wife had appeared. Dad slapped me across the face and punched me in the kidneys. 'I told you to be fucking good, didn't I?' he said, leaving me crying as he stormed off.

When Mum came home, my face was still red. She saw it when I got up for a glass of water and asked me what had happened. Dad told her I'd fallen, and she tutted as usual, as if I was a terrible burden to her, then asked how much babysitting money I'd earned. I said I'd got nothing but Dad butted in again to say that he'd get the cash from Billy in the halfway house next time he saw him. The signal was obvious to me – if I was good I got the money, if I wasn't, I didn't.

I realised I was trapped – there was no way out of this.

The next time I went to Billy's house, it was obvious he and Dad had been talking. I didn't know how much he was aware of what happened between me and Dad; was my own father telling other men about the secret? The night before I went to babysit, Dad had sat me down 'to have a word'.

'Billy is my friend,' he said, 'and, more importantly, he's a good man, a good soldier. Don't you dare embarrass me ever again. If he wants you to help him out, then that's exactly what you'll do.'

So my continued abuse by another 'good man' was to be acceptable because it would save my dad from embarrassment and help Billy Stoppard out? As I lay there that night, with my own father raping me yet again, I wondered what the future would be for Billy's three little girls, the ones I supposedly babysat. Would they be sold on to my dad when they got older? One of them was only a year younger than I had been when he had started on me – were they facing the same destiny?

Dad frequently had a lot of porn around the house and I always felt he probably traded it with his friends as I would see packages being passed between them. I think that was one of the reasons he kept us out of the cellar and wouldn't let us use it as a den the way other kids did. I believe it was his storeroom for lots of things. The first time I knew of him having magazines like that was when I came home one day and Gary was acting strangely. Mum was out cleaning and Dad was still at work, and my brother had been raking around in their bedroom looking for Christmas presents. He'd been shuffling through things in their wardrobe when a stash of porn fell out. Although he thought of himself as tough, Gary had quite a sheltered life really. He was never hit and Mum treated him as if he was five years old. If he had seen porn before (and I guess there would be mags being passed around between teenage boys at that time as they didn't have the internet), it was probably pretty tame stuff – but this wasn't. It was hard core, and it had obviously shocked Gary a bit. When I asked what was wrong, he avoided telling me for a while, then said, 'Come and see what I've found.' He wasn't full of bravado or showing off, he seemed genuinely puzzled and shaken.

In some ways the pictures didn't have the same effect on me because an awful lot of those things had been done to me since I was a little girl. However, I had never seen them so explicitly. It was like looking at a catalogue of my own abuse. I completely related it to what was done to me, and I assumed these women were all in the same position as me. Maybe they were, I have no idea if it was consensual or not. Whatever the legality of it all, I was amazed there were images like that. As Gary flicked through, I saw one photograph of a woman kneeling down masturbating a man – I was drawn to it because I had never really envisaged what the reality of that act was when I was being forced into it. I didn't even know that grown-ups did those things – I thought they were part of the special secret between daddies and little girls to keep mummies out of hospital.

From that moment on, the knowledge that my dad had those magazines haunted me. Although he never showed them to me or left them lying around openly, I could always find them easily and the fact that they existed confused me. Why were other people doing these things? The women in the pictures were grown-ups – I couldn't understand if the men in the pictures were their daddies or, if not, what their dads would think about them doing such things. Wouldn't they get into terrible trouble? Every time I saw Dad passing magazines or books to other men in the pub, I would wonder whether they were full of pictures like the ones Gary had found.

Once I started 'babysitting', I was even more terrified of going to the halfway house to collect Dad than I had been in the past. Too many times, Billy Stoppard was there and I saw him leering at me whenever I came in. He was often passing magazines to the others. I once asked Dad what they were and he just said 'car mags', but I didn't know if that was the truth and I had less reason to believe it once Billy Stoppard decided to show me some of his collection.

One night when I was at his house, instead of trying to get me in the kitchen or at the door, he told me to wait a minute before I left. One of his kids had fallen asleep on the sofa, so I didn't want to leave until I was sure he was looking after them properly.

He went into another room and came back with a magazine. He sat down beside me on the sofa – far too close – and said he wanted to show me something nice. That worried me – men who said that to me had very different ideas

154

about what was 'nice'. He brought out a magazine and opened it to a photograph of two naked women touching each other in their private places. 'Look,' he said, 'isn't that nice?' I tried to get off the sofa, but he pulled me back down. 'I need to go,' I said, 'my dad will be wondering about where I am.'

He laughed. 'Don't you worry about that – I think your dad doesn't mind at all that you're here with me, Tracy.'

That was exactly what worried me.

'Look,' he kept saying, 'they're having a good time, aren't they?'

I turned my head away; I didn't want to see or to have him watching me while I did.

I heard him flicking the pages. 'Oh, here's a lovely one,' he said. 'I like this. Do you like it?'

Again, I refused to turn my head. He grabbed my arm at the top and nipped me. I didn't move. His hand moved to my leg and started rubbing it. 'Tracy? Look. I want you to look. I really do think you should look.'

There was a threat in his voice – and I'd rather look at his filthy magazines than have him touch me. I looked. It was what seemed to be a Polaroid picture in the mag, an actual photograph of what I thought of as 'real' people. A woman was kneeling down in front of a man and they both had their eyes blackened out. She had his penis in her mouth. 'Just think, Tracy,' Billy said, 'that could be you.'

I jumped up off the sofa and ran to the door – I had no idea how long I could keep fighting him off.

CHAPTER 16

STILL THE GOOD GIRL

The answer was, not long.

The next time I went to Billy and Chrissie's, she wasn't there and he was. It looked as if even the usual pretence of him working was to be discarded. The kids were already in bed and I walked through to the kitchen as soon as he opened the door to me.

I went to go and check on his children, but he stopped me. 'No need – they're asleep. I think it's time you and I had a little chat, Tracy, don't you?'

He held me by the elbow and guided me to the kitchen table. 'If you don't need me here tonight, Mr Stoppard, I'll just head back home,' I said.

'I don't think so,' he replied. 'I'm a bit confused, Tracy. You see, I thought you were a good girl. Your dad tells me you're a good girl. In fact, in the pub, your dad tells all of his friends that you're a good girl.' My heart sank. I had suspected this but I hadn't wanted to have it confirmed. 'So, Tracy, I think it's time for you to prove he is right – it's time for you to be a good girl.'

Sitting at that table, where he presumably ate breakfast with his wife and children, that horrible man unzipped his trousers and exposed himself. 'You know what to do,' he told me, 'I know you do.'

I actually wasn't sure what he meant but I knew it was one of only two options – he either wanted me to use my hand or my mouth and, after the experience with my dad, I knew I would gag if it was the latter. I hated myself for it, but in order to prevent him forcing me to use my mouth, I masturbated him. He touched me throughout but it thankfully didn't last for long. As soon as it was over, he stroked me on the cheek and told me I was a good girl. 'Can I go now?' I asked. 'Of course you can.' I picked up my coat and went towards the door.

'Tracy!' he called. 'You haven't done the babysitting and I'm letting you off early, but take this anyway.' He threw ten Deutschmarks at me in a gesture of generosity. How kind – I hadn't looked after his kids but I had been a good girl and provided him with sexual release. Dad would be so proud. I took the money – I still wanted to go on the skiing trip – and left.

Dad wasn't in when I got home, but the next night he came back from the pub and came into my room. 'Good girl,' he said, 'well done.' He left without another word.

This happened a few times and moved on to Billy Stoppard cuddling me before I masturbated him. He also started touching me between the legs just as Dad did. I was still getting abused at home during this time too – it never seemed to stop. 'You're a good girl,' Dad would tell me after he or Billy had done what they wanted, 'you're my good girl. You're Daddy's girl and your mum will be all right now.'

But she wasn't. Her health was heading downhill fast and she wasn't getting any better, no matter how many awful things I did with horrible men. The next time I was at Billy's house, he told me to take my dress off. There was something about that suggestion that worried me – I thought back to the photographs and magazines he had shown me and wondered whether he would be getting a camera out.

I refused.

It had been a while since I had done that and I think he was quite shocked. 'Are you kidding?' he asked. 'Since when do you get to call the shots?'

'I don't want to, I just don't want to.'

'Tough. Get over here or I'll tell your dad what an awkward little bitch you are.'

For once in my life, I had a stroke of luck. I heard the door open and Chrissie come in. Billy shot up to give her an excuse about mixing up his work times and I took the opportunity to leave. I never went back.

When I got home, Dad was waiting. 'Where's your babysitting money?' he asked. This was code – he knew if I'd been paid by Billy, then I had allowed him to abuse me and my dad could hold his head high in the pub that week, secure in the knowledge that his little girl had done him proud.

'There's no money and I'm not going back,' I told him defiantly.

'Is that right?'

He stormed off – presumably to the pub to find out from Billy what had happened. When he came back, he came straight into my room and took my piggy bank. Without a word, he emptied out all of the money I'd saved. He left the room and shouted to my brother. 'Gary! How do you fancy going on that skiing trip? Your sister isn't keen any more.' I heard Gary whoop with joy as my dad twisted the knife in further. 'Here, take this for spending money.' The Deutschmarks I had earned in such a horrific way were handed over just like that.

I couldn't even cry any more. Maybe Dad was right; maybe I was a prostitute. I also started to believe again what he had always told me about my collusion determining Mum's health because, after standing up to Billy Stoppard, she was taken into hospital in a state worse than she had been for many years. This time one of her ulcers had been awful. I could smell the paraffin oil that she used when things got bad and she was losing an awful amount of weight as she couldn't keep anything down. The physical and sexual abuse got worse when she was in hospital and my dad must have known it was rape, because I spent every episode crying, struggling, and telling him I didn't want it.

Dad was still going to the pub a lot, when he wasn't drinking at home, and he was still getting me to meet him there some nights. The situation which had occurred with Billy Stoppard wasn't the only time I was sent to places to 'babysit' with the sole purpose of putting me in the hands of men who wanted to abuse me. I was in no doubt I was being asked to come to the pub to be shown off to men who would be interested in doing the same. It was like some sort of perverted audition in front of a group of paedophiles.

There was one guy who was part of the group there who I had actually heard of in the base. He was notorious among the kids. He was called Norman Parker and had four kids of his own. He was a good bit older than my dad, maybe fifteen years older; I knew that because he was on his way out of the Army. He was higher up than my dad and in a different regiment – this in itself was telling, as usually the ranks stuck to being mates with people on the same level as them. The more I've thought about this while writing this book, the more I've realised that the group in the pub cut across all ages, backgrounds and ranks; but they were close. There was clearly something binding them, a common interest or mutual hobby.

On this one night when I had turned up to meet my dad at his request, I was standing by the side of his table as usual (I was never invited to sit and would have felt just as uncomfortable doing that anyway) when Norman Parker appeared from the toilets. There was a drink waiting for him at the table and as he approached, he shouted out, 'Who do we have here then, Harry?' The fact that he asked my dad, by name, again suggested to me that they had all been talking about me before I got there. Now they were seeing me in the flesh, so to speak.

'I told you I had a daughter,' Dad replied. 'This is her. This is Tracy.' They all knew he had a daughter anyway, they knew us from the base, but this didn't sound like him giving out information, this sounded like him presenting me in a different way, as something for them to consider.

'Oh,' said Norman, 'you'll like it at my house. You can play with my kiddies. All the kiddies like it there.'

I knew exactly what he was talking about – he wasn't referring to his own brood as they were all older than me, he was meaning the huge gang of children who always hung around his cellar. 'You'll have to come round, have some fun,' he continued.

My response was immediate. 'No thanks.'

He looked at me seriously, then at my dad. 'Harry, I said she'll have to come round, won't she?'

'Yes. Yes, she will,' Dad confirmed.

'That's settled then,' said Norman. 'I'll see you at the play den tomorrow.' All of the men around the table laughed.

The next day, a weekend, Dad got me out of bed early. 'Come on,' he told me, 'you're going to Norman's today.'

'I am not,' I replied.

'You fucking are. I won't be shown up again, so get out of your pit and get washed.'

There was no arguing but I had no intention of just doing whatever that horrible man wanted me to once I got to his 'play den'.

The house was a tip. Mrs Parker was huge and spent all day eating if gossip was to believed. The kids weren't wild exactly, but she didn't give a toss about them. And Mr Parker? He spent all day in his cellar playing games with the local kids and reading. I had heard from others that you could always get porn there, and I had also heard that he liked to play particular games. The stories I had been told about Norman Parker had shocked me – no one knew more than me that men with unnatural interests in children existed, but I had never heard it spoken about so openly.

When I got there, he already had a lot of children in his garden. There were bikes and toys everywhere, and he left them out constantly – I could only think that was to lure kids in. What I couldn't understand was, if there was all this talk about him, why did other parents let their children go there unsupervised? I knew why my dad allowed it, but surely not every child there had a pervert for a parent?

Norman was all over the kids. He would chase them and play hide and seek, he would tickle them and throw them up in the air. It was obvious to me what was happening, I recognised the signs and had a sense of it. I was terrified I would get drawn into it too – I also felt that, if Parker was accepted, then it would be even harder for me to get away as so many people seemed to let him get away with whatever he was doing.

On that first day, he didn't touch me. He seemed content to just let me watch what went on and was keen to keep emphasising how much fun everyone had, how much all the local kids liked being there. I didn't tell him what they said about him behind his back.

A few days later, Dad said I was to go back. He took me as he said he had a book to exchange with Norman. When we got there, the book was handed over and Dad left. 'Come on,' said Norman, 'let me show you my play den.' We went down to the cellar and, again, there were toys everywhere. He had lots of bookshelves lining the walls and bowls of sweets lying around. There were also lots of camp beds, lined up in an L-shape and covered in dirty sheets, with stains on them like shoe prints. In fact, the whole place was filthy.

I realised I was the only other person there – no one else was in the cellar or the garden. Other children had done these areas up as their spaces, but this was clearly his territory. Everything was laid out, as it was in the garden, to tempt children. Action Man dolls, tricycles, sledges, balls, dolls, teddies, board games – it was like an Aladdin's cave. My alarm bells had been ringing since the first time I had met him – I was getting smarter and I had been abused enough to know the signs – but I had no idea who I could or would tell about this. Everyone seemed to be blind to him – or perhaps they just didn't care. Why was no one asking why this man had all of this lying about when his own children were far too old for it?

As I looked around, he spoke. 'Fancy a piggyback?'

'What?' I asked.

'Do you fancy a piggyback?'

'No,' I replied. 'Why would I?'

'It might be fun – it would be fun,' he replied. 'You can have sweets. You can have as many sweets as you like.'

'I don't want sweets and I don't want a piggyback. Actually, I want to go home.'

'Well, you can't. Your dad said you've to be a good girl.'

I was sick of this. I was sick of being passed from man to man like an insignificant little toy. He was suddenly distracted by the sound of some children coming downstairs and I went to sit on a garden chair in the sun. If I had to stay, I'd keep away from him.

He was easily distracted and I managed to spend the rest of the day without having to talk to him again. When I got home, Dad asked whether I had been good. The code again. I ignored him and went to my room. I had stood up to Billy Stoppard and I would do so to Norman Parker.

'Your mum's in hospital and we both know it's because of you,' Dad said, storming in. You'll go to Norman's again and you'll do as you're fucking told.' He stood there waiting for a response. I think the fact that I wasn't scared into making a commitment was probably a shock to him.

The next time I was taken there, I had been thinking about mum in hospital. The threat didn't have the same power as it used to but I did still wonder whether there was anything I could do to make her better. It's hard to break away from that sort of conditioning, even when, in retrospect, you can see how ridiculous it was.

Again, Norman offered me a piggyback ride, but this time when I refused he walked over to me and picked me up. I was kicking my legs, but the garden was full, which made me unwilling to create a scene but also had me wondering whether he would have the nerve to try anything with an audience around him. He did. His hands were holding on to my buttocks and his fingers were getting closer and closer to my knickers. I tried to kick him harder but it made no difference. He was laughing and running around the garden with me, and still trying to stick his fingers up inside me – he had clearly had a lot of practice. I dug my nails into the back of his neck, which must have surprised him as he gave a little yelp and dropped me onto the grass.

For the rest of the morning, Norman sat on a garden chair, smoking and watching everyone. He was a scruffy, slobbish man, unlike my dad, and he kept scratching himself as he sat there. His youngest boy was there that day, although he was older than me, and he was playing hide and seek with two girls. The girls went off to hide and Norman came over to me. 'Right, we're it – you'll have to help.'

I pointed to his son. 'No, he's it and I don't want to.'

The boy was watching his father and ran off immediately. Norman grabbed my hand and said, 'Join in – it'll be fun.' He pulled me behind a hedge and started to grope me, but I wasn't having any of it. His hands were all over me in seconds and I felt sick at the idea of having yet another monster pawing me. I ran for the gate as he shouted, 'I'll tell your dad!' I didn't care. I'd rather take the beating than what that horrible man had planned for me.

I went home and tried to work out what I'd say to Dad. When I got in, he was just putting the phone down. 'What's wrong?' I asked, looking at the worry on his face.

'It's your mum,' he replied. This is it, I thought. She's dead, and it's all because of me. 'She's worse – they need to move her.'

The doctors had decided to ship her back to the UK. They still didn't know what was wrong with her but were getting very worried about the cumulative effects of the illness; her vital signs were down and even the intravenous drip wasn't working as well as they'd hoped. Later that week, just as summer started, Dad announced with no warning that he couldn't look after me and Gary any more. We were to be sent off to his family back in Scotland. Gary ranted and raved about this, but I was delighted. I didn't know Dad's folks very well, but anything was better than what I was living in.

Gary went to stay with one auntie, I went to another. Dad came with us for a few days and stayed with the sister who had Gary. When he travelled back to Germany, he didn't even bother to come and say goodbye to me. I didn't care. From the moment I arrived at my Auntie Dee's, it was heaven. It was during the summer holidays so I had no school to worry about and it was such a relief to get away from home. That summer, 1973, in Scotland was my release. I got the chance to be a normal kid.

Auntie Dee had four kids and she loved them all. It was a revelation for me. All my cousins had loads of friends and I was just accepted as one of them. We went to the local youth club, played pool, attempted tennis, listened to music, danced – nothing unusual for most kids, but another world for me. I was even noticing that some boys were nice. I had always been told to keep away from boys, by both Mum and Dad, but he in particular had said they were bad and dirty and only after one thing. *They'll never love you properly*, he told me, *not like I do.*

I was so distanced from my horrible real life while I was

there that I realised the truth of my relationship with my mum too. Now I was away and could see things more clearly, I really didn't give a damn about her. When I was little, my concern was for having my mum there all the time, but she'd been so horrible to me and I'd suffered such things for her, I didn't really care any more. I gave up on her – but she had given up on me long before that.

Seeing how my Auntie Dee was with her kids opened my eyes – she was loving and caring, and always had time for each one. She would play with them, come out and muck about in the garden, have a game of football, cuddle them all constantly, do the garden so she always had rhubarb to make crumble; everything was connected to them. She was always teaching them and thinking of them. My Uncle Freddie was great too. He would sit and explain homework to the kids when they went back to school, why they had to do it and how it would help them. I got to see a lovely alternative while I was there. Dad left me with Auntie Dee so long that her kids went back to school after the six-week break and I got to be with her on my own. I'll always treasure that time.

It ended all too soon. I got word that my mum was being sent back to Germany to convalesce and my summer was over. I had never really given her another thought until that moment and then the dread began. When I thought about the abuse starting all over, I had panic attacks. Auntie Dee would sit with me while I breathed into a brown paper bag. 'What's the matter, hen?' she'd ask. 'What's getting you so worked up?' I did think of telling her, but I just couldn't. She was a lovely woman, but the thought of informing her that her own brother was a paedophile who regularly raped his own daughter was something I couldn't force myself to say.

It was time to find my voice – when I got home.

CHAPTER 17

STARTING THE FIRE

Mum had been moved to a German hospital and Gary and I went back to school. To begin with, when I returned, my resolve faltered. As soon as I got home, Dad said to me: 'Have you any idea how ill your mum is? It's been touch and go.' He was sending me a clear message and the abuse began all over again. However, this time I had decided that, even if I couldn't stop him, I was determined not to make it easy. Every time he touched me, I told him the same things. I didn't want this. I hated it. He was doing it against my will. The biggest change of all though was the final threat I lobbed at him – I was going to tell Mum.

'Do you want to kill her? Do you want that on your fucking conscience?' he asked, shocked, but this wasn't affecting me in the same way any more. By the time I was twelve, I had something else to throw at him. Every time he raped me, I got the most awful pains in my stomach, which I decided to use to my tiny advantage too. 'I think I'm starting my period,' I told him.

'You better fucking not, I won't have it,' he told me, as if either of us could stop it. I could see he was rattled. He didn't want me to grow up, I knew that. As I got taller, older, he would say to me that I was changing, that I wasn't his little girl any more, and I could see this was a bad thing for him. He didn't want me to talk back or fight back, and he didn't want me turning into a woman. It was a child he wanted to terrorise.

I wasn't given to any other men when I got back from Scotland but there was another threat which I hadn't even anticipated. Gary had been nasty to me for years, for as long as I could remember really. He bullied me a lot, pulled my hair, kicked me whenever he got the chance – in some ways, this wasn't surprising. He had seen casual violence being dished out to me since I was so little, and he had also seen there were never any consequences for the perpetrator of that violence. On top of that, he had been going to karate classes for years as it was another way for Dad to get him out of the house, so he was much stronger than me and was always trying out his stupid moves when I was least prepared.

One day, after Dad had stormed out of the house, I was in my bedroom tidying up. Almost before I knew what was happening, Gary came up behind me, grabbed my neck and did something. I don't know what he did, but it was so powerful it knocked me out. When I came to, he was standing over me with a stupid grin on his face.

'What on earth did you do?' I asked.

He just laughed at me and walked out.

This happened again about a week later, but then a few days after that he came into my room while Dad was out and sat on my bed.

'I know what you've been doing,' he said.

'What are you talking about?' I asked.

'Think about it – you've been doing something you shouldn't have been doing, and I know all about it.'

My heart sank. Did he know? Did he really know what Dad had been doing to me for years? Just as these thoughts were going through my head, he grabbed me and pulled me into the bed. He punched me in the stomach and twisted my hair and then tried to climb on top of me. I could feel his body react to mine in the same way my father's did. The panting started, the heavy breathing, and I knew he was getting excited. I fought against him and got strength from somewhere – I couldn't let this happen again in my own home, with my own brother. I scratched and kicked and bit him, and he finally jumped off. Did he come to his senses or did he realise I wasn't going to give in easily? I have no idea.

This all really shook me – and it provided the catalyst I needed to try and get someone to notice what was going on. My behaviour became much worse and I was attention-seeking constantly. I was also often at the doctors with cystitis, despite being so young. (I was just given sachets of some medicine to take without so much as an examination.) I was excluded from lots of normal things; I chose to be naughty whenever I could, but still no one was picking up on any of it.

I had started smoking years earlier, as part of my plan to be accepted by older kids. I was getting a reputation for being tough, not a particularly accurate one as it was only based on me wearing boyish clothes, DMs, and always having a packet of fags in my pocket.

The windows had all been put in the new houses on the estate I had previously been to, and I had a plan. One Saturday afternoon, I arranged to go there with a boy called Liam, who was the year ahead of me at school. There was nothing between us other than friendship as I couldn't bear to think of boys that way. As I was a smoker, I always had matches with me, so I suggested to Liam that we build a fire. He wasn't too sure and didn't know why I would want to do that, but I persuaded him that if we started it in a bath it would be safe – and if anyone saw us, I'd take all the blame. I don't think he believed I would, but what he didn't know was that I didn't want to share or deflect the blame – it was all about getting attention for me and hoping someone would notice why I needed it in the first place.

I set the fire, with Liam just watching. There was a lot of rubbish lying around the site so there was no shortage of material. While it was taking hold, I started to do some graffiti, drawing Union Jacks on the wall with the ashes. Liam went outside to have a cigarette and I was distracted by my 'art'. When he came back he shouted, 'Tracy! It's getting out of control!' I looked round, and he was right – the fire was blazing. I told him to get help but he was too worried, so I reiterated that I would take the blame. While he went off to find a call box – there were no mobile phones back then – I tried to dampen it down with water but it wasn't helping.

I waited for help, not even thinking of leaving as that would defeat my plan, and eventually the police came. At first they started quizzing me in German, but soon switched to English once I started talking. I admitted it all to them, and they said someone else must have been there because of all the cigarette butts lying around; however, I kept to my word and didn't mention Liam.

I was taken home by the police, which was the third time they had been involved. They didn't prosecute for all the damage I'd caused as Dad offered to pay for it – again, that was him trying to prevent our family being looked at too closely. Also, he wouldn't only be putting himself in the firing line if someone investigated our family, he would also be threatening to reveal the sickening secrets of others.

The German police officers accepted that Dad would pay and no charges brought, but as they now knew I had been in trouble a few times they said something had to be done or they would be forced to report me to the British military police; as things were, they were going to have to send a report to the Army anyway. They said a social worker would have to be called, which Dad reacted against immediately. However, he hadn't accounted for my mum, who was all for it. He had to agree. Before I met the social worker for the first time, he made sure I knew the rules.

'You say nothing,' he told me. 'You don't tell her how you manage to keep your mum out of hospital because she won't understand. Lots of little girls have these secrets with their daddies, but people like the social worker wouldn't know what to make of it and they would just think you were bad. She'll make it all worse if you tell her and your mum will die.' He urged me to say I had got in with a bad crowd and they had encouraged me to do all the things the police were aware of. I know he was worried the social worker would sense something and start picking at the dysfunctional threads of our family life, but he needn't have lost any sleep over it; she was a silly cow who was only in the job for the money as far as I could see.

Her name was Mrs Walker. She was very short and fat, with a strong Liverpudlian accent. She often wore her hair stretched as tightly back as possible and dressed in plain clothes in dull colours. I once saw her files, which had the letters SSAF and BFSWS on them – the first stood for Social Services Army Forces (it's an acronym used for a charitable group now) and the second was British Forces Social Work Services.

On the first scheduled visit, she came to our house. Within minutes, my mum stood up to leave the room, muttering one of her favourite excuses – 'I can't handle this'. She left Dad to deal with it all, as he must have wanted to do anyway, and he suggested Mrs Walker and I have our meetings elsewhere in future to avoid distressing my 'very ill' mother. They decided she would pick me up from school when she needed to have an appointment with me, and take me to a café then bring me back home. I'd had so much hope for this woman and felt that, if she was the right person, I could and would confide in her, but throughout that first meeting, she didn't even talk to me.

Dad had prepared me with a script really – I was to say the things about bullies at school getting me into bad ways, that I was upset about Mum being in hospital a lot, that Gary kept hitting me. The latter was actually true – he had seen Dad doing it for years and had started lashing out at me since we got back to Germany as well as those occasions when he had tried to force himself on me. My Dad just had a lucky guess with that one, but I could say it happened to Mrs Walker in all honesty. We spent two hours together for each of the twelve weeks allocated and during that time she gave me no reason to think she was remotely interested in the truth.

She asked me the same things every time about how my day had gone at school. I had been given conduct cards for teachers to fill in and she collected these from me, discussing what was on them. I behaved at school though. I liked it and didn't skip off. When we only had a few weeks left she asked her first perceptive question.

'Do you know what I'm going to ask you every week, Tracy?'

'Yes,' I replied, 'you always ask me the same things.'

'Don't be so cheeky,' she snapped. 'I mean … well, you always seem to have your answers almost prepared.'

I waited for her to say more. It wouldn't have taken someone with enormous brainpower to work out why that was the case. I was tempted to tell her she was an idiot even at that young age.

'You need to be good. Do you think you can be a good girl?' she asked, obviously bored.

Of course I could. I'd been doing it for years, but when I was getting into trouble, I was choosing to get into trouble and no one was asking why.

I knew time was running out so at our next meeting, when we were driving to a café and she asked me if I could be good, I gave Mrs Walker an answer she hadn't been expecting.

'I know why I've been naughty,' I told her.

'Really?' she answered, looking interested for the first time.

I took a deep breath and closed my eyes as the words finally came out.

'It's my dad. My dad's been touching me. He touches me and hurts me and does bad things to me and I want it to stop.'

She nearly crashed the car as she stared at me. 'Don't say such terrible things, Tracy! What an awful excuse to give for your appalling behaviour.'

'But Mrs Walker,' I insisted, 'it's true, he does do things to me.'

'It's utterly ridiculous to even think of such a thing. Your father is right – you're a very bad girl indeed.' She regained her composure and started driving again as if nothing had happened.

Was that it? I had waited for years to say something and, now that I had, the person who was meant to help me, whose *job* it was to help me, was just going to brush it aside?

We carried on to the café where Mrs Walker filled in that week's forms. She said nothing to me and I know she didn't write it in her report as they were given to my parents and the shit never did hit the fan. When she dropped me off at home that day, she informed me there was no point in continuing with the sessions as I was clearly intent on being naughty.

That was it.

That was my one attempt to tell someone and it didn't work.

Her response had made me so angry. I felt so betrayed that the adult who should have at least been professional and considered what I had alleged had ignored me. I promised myself I would tell again, I would keep telling until someone listened, and the next person I told would have more invested than a cold-hearted social worker.

The next person I told would be my mum.

CHAPTER 18

GETTING OUT

When Mum got back from hospital after our return from Scotland, she was definitely much better than she had been for years, which wasn't surprising as she'd been in for so long, but something had happened between her and Dad. They had never been a loving couple but they seemed to be arguing a lot more than was usual even for them.

I knew their adult relationship wasn't as it should be for many reasons. Not only had my dad put me in Mum's place sexually, but she was suspicious of him. Each time her illness got worse she would get terrible blisters and ulcers all over her body. One time, I heard them talking in their bedroom and they were arguing because Mum had them on her genitals. Mum said to him, 'If you've given me anything, I'll leave you – that's it, I'll walk.'

'Don't be stupid,' he told her. 'I haven't been near anyone else.'

That was obviously a lie; he never had his hands off me. Maybe I didn't count.

'Well, I can't remember the last time you touched me,' she countered.

I knew more by now. I was twelve, I was hanging around older kids a lot and there was plenty of talk about sex. From my completely inappropriate experience, I knew that lots of what they said was inaccurate, but I was also piecing things together and making sense of the things which had been done to me since I was five. My parents' conversation showed me they weren't sleeping together and she was willing to suspect him of being with someone else.

There was lots of niggling going on between them about petty things too. Mum had a radiogram that she loved and she had her own particular records which she played over and over again. During this time, he went on at her a lot about playing Sandie Shaw constantly as he said he was sick of listening to it. They didn't argue exactly, he just told her she was to stop. He commandeered the radiogram and made sure his music was on all the time – he still liked things such as Frank Sinatra and Johnny Cash, crooners were his sort of thing, and he 'allowed' Mum a few listens to people like more modern singers such as Dusty Springfield, who didn't annoy him too much.

The atmosphere was even worse than I was used to, but I still couldn't pluck up the courage to tell Mum. I decided to run away instead. That night, I started preparing my things with the plan of leaving soon. Gary came into my room and asked what I was doing. I told him the truth, that I was getting ready to leave, as I knew he wouldn't tell – I reasoned he would prefer it if I wasn't there. He left the room for a few moments and returned with a couple of my records – I wasn't going to pack those, but I thought he was maybe just making a nice gesture.

'Are you going away because you told?' he asked.

'Yes.'

'Did you tell on me?' he asked, worriedly.

'No, Mum wouldn't ever believe that.' It was the truth. 'She'd blame that on me as well.'

'Tracy – I don't want to be like him. I know what he does to you.'

'Please don't tell anyone, Gary,' I pleaded. I was still scared that Mum would get ill if everyone knew.

'I won't – but you have to tell me what he does when you're alone together.'

'I thought you knew?'

'Well, I do – but I need to hear it from you.'

Did he know everything for sure or did he just have suspicions? I have no idea but he wanted me to elaborate.

'Does he touch you in private places?'

'Does he make you touch him in private places?'

'Does he make you kiss him down there?'

'Does he make you suck it?'

'Does he put it in you?'

YES, YES, YES, my head was screaming, but I could only nod.

'Don't tell anyone or Mum will die,' I said.

'Will she?' he asked, thoughtfully. 'OK, I'll keep it a secret. I won't tell – but Tracy? You have to do what you do to him. You have to touch me.'

I couldn't believe this. He had been so understanding at first, seemingly so supportive, but now, instead of consoling me, he just wanted to use it as an excuse to abuse me too.

He made me masturbate him that day and then, about a week later, waited until we were in the house alone and then shouted through from his bedroom. 'Sis, come here. I need you to do something for me.' I went through and he was sitting there with his penis out. Like father, like son. He tried to rape me that day but I fought him off again and he graciously accepted that his twelve-year-old traumatised little sister masturbate him instead. He warned me that if I said anything he would batter and kill me.

Gary had mood swings just like Dad. He was all over the place with how he behaved from one day to the next – and the following morning, he put his arm out to stop me leaving the kitchen. 'About yesterday ...' he said. 'I'm sorry, Tracy. I'm really sorry.' He shook his head then moved his arm away. 'I'll never have kids.'

Gary kept to his word and had a vasectomy when he was twenty. In some ways this was odd, because of the rumours that he wasn't my dad's biological child, but only he would know the feelings he had, and perhaps the socialisation he had been provided with in his childhood with Dad as a role model was enough to make him fear what he might become. (It was interesting that when he told my mum of his plans she immediately complained she would never have grandchildren, ignoring the fact that she had a daughter even then.)

This was all too much.

I waited until Dad was working and Gary was at a sleep-over. I knew by now that Mum would never love me the way I needed her to, the way all children need their mothers to, but I had to tell her what had been happening for the past seven years. She was my only hope now. I must be honest and admit that, in my heart, I dreamed of a moment when she would realise all I had done for her and everything would work out.

'Mum, can I have a word?' I asked, as she sat watching telly.

'If you must,' she replied, not taking her eyes off the screen.

'I've got something I need to talk to you about …' I began. 'It's a bit difficult …'

'Have you been messing with boys?' she snapped.

'No! Well, it's that sort of thing, but … this is really hard.'

'Well, hurry up, will you? I don't have all night.'

She did have all night. She was only glued to the TV, wishing she was at bingo. I didn't know how to get the words out – I had to tell her things I never wanted to speak of, never wanted to verbalise. She was in a hurry, she wanted me out of the room and she wanted to be left alone to watch soap operas and brain-numbing game shows.

I wanted to turn around and leave, to mutter that it didn't matter, but it *did* matter.

'Mum, it's about Dad.'

'What about your dad?'

What were the words I could use? How could I say the

things which would change all our lives forever? I had to just get it over and done with.

'He's been doing things to me. He's been touching me. He's been touching me in ways he shouldn't for years, Mum.'

She still stared at the television.

'Rubbish,' was her only comment.

I took a deep breath.

'It isn't rubbish, it's the truth. Since I was five, he's told me that I have to do these things to keep you out of hospital and that's why I have. I loved you so much, Mum, and I'd have done anything to make you well.'

I waited for a response but there was absolutely nothing coming from her.

'Mum? Have you heard anything I've said?'

'I've heard it.'

'Mum! He raped me! Dad's been raping me!'

She turned to face me and stood up slowly, pointing a finger at me. '*HE* is my husband. *YOU* are only my daughter. It's all lies. Go away.'

That was it. She sat back down and stared at the screen. I fled to my room and started to sob. I should have known. She had never felt anything for me and she was bound to my dad. There may have been no love between them but he had looked after her financially all these years, provided her with a home and security, been there through all her illness. What was I to her? A burden. If she had believed what I had said, it would have blown apart what there was of our family life and she couldn't risk that. What could I do now? I had been thinking of running away for weeks, and had been preparing for it; I knew now that was my only option.

Before I had stayed with Auntie Dee, I hadn't questioned things so much, but that had given me a different view on family life. She would have killed for her kids and if any of them had told her what I had just told my mum, she would have protected them against everything. I had seen something outside my bubble while I lived with her and I wanted that, I didn't want my family's perverted version of normality.

I ran away that night. Mum hadn't spoken to me again and I stayed in my room when Gary and Dad came back. I planned to go to my friend Holly and tell her I was leaving. When I got there, I had whittled down the things in my backpack to what really mattered to me and had little more than my DMs and an extra jacket. I was frightened but I didn't think I had any other options.

When I told Holly I was running away, she naturally asked why. I wasn't ready to tell everyone the full extent of what had been going on so I said Dad had been hitting me.

'So?' she said. 'My dad hits me all the time.'

'Well, I don't like it and my mum's hardly ever there,' I told her.

'You can't run away. Where would you go?' she pointed out. 'Stay here and go back tomorrow. They'll have been so worried about you that they'll be nice. At least they will for a while.' She said it with such certainty that I wondered whether she had tried it herself at times. 'You can spend the night in our cellar.'

Holly's den was nice. She had soft furnishings and a sofa bed. There were lots of lamps made out of 1960s fibreglass. It was a windy night and I didn't sleep much. I had asked Holly to keep my presence a secret from her parents and she stuck to her word. The next morning she wanted to know if I was going home. When I said I wasn't, she said she couldn't hide me for another night as her mum would get suspicious, so I went to the house of a girl called Gillian Harrison. I told Gillian the same story about Dad hitting me and she also suggested I bunk down in the cellar for the night.

The day after that, I went back to Holly, who asked me if I had gone home yet. 'No,' I answered. 'Why would I?'

'Well, your dad came looking for you at my house,' she said. 'Your mum is really ill again. I thought he'd found you and taken you back. I'm sure he won't hit you now, he'll be too upset about your mum.'

She knew nothing. The old pull still had its hold on me though and, reluctantly, I went home. Dad laid into me as soon as I got in and told me I was too late, Mum had been taken into hospital that morning. I didn't think she had said anything to him about my revelation because he wouldn't have been able to keep that back when he was shouting at me.

That night, I wished I was back in Holly or Gillian's cellars. I wouldn't care about the wind or the cold, I would happily stay awake all night there because at least I would be safe. Dad came into my bed and told me how selfish I was, and, my body bruised once more from his attacks, I ran away that night again.

I spent the night at Gillian's, and didn't go to school the next day. I'd had a lot of time to think and one thing which kept going around in my mind was what Dad was going to do next. What was there *left* for him to do? I was stuck. I dreaded the idea of going back but I had no money and very few friends I could stay with. I went back home that night and Mum was home. She hadn't been in hospital long but he hadn't even mentioned to her that I'd been away.

He collared me that night as I was going to the kitchen for a drink.

'Don't you even think of playing up again,' he said. 'You stay here. You don't play at running away. You do every single thing I fucking tell you.'

'Or what?' I retorted.

'You know what – your mum will get ill and she might die.'

I laughed in his face. It was the first time I had ever done that.

'Don't bother, Dad,' I said. 'I've worked that one out.'

He looked at me as if I'd slapped him.

'And I'll tell her. I'll tell her everything.'

By his reaction of shock, I knew Mum definitely hadn't said anything to him about me already telling her. He moved forward and had the audacity to try and hug me, but something had changed. I pushed him away and went to my room, slamming the door behind me.

What had given me that strength? The times I had run away. The fact that I had survived on my own. The realisation that my mum didn't care about me or believe me. The fact that he didn't even try to change the lies he told me and kept on with the same ones he had used for seven whole years. And the overriding image of my Auntie Dee and her family, who had given me the belief that things could be different.

I had lost so much. When I heard girls talking about boys, when my cousins had chatted about their first kiss or holding hands with the ones they loved, and even when the older ones spoke about how they wanted the first time to be special, I had realised just how much my dad had ripped from me. I'd never get any of that back again, but I could stop it all right now. I had a voice and I was going to start shouting.

I grabbed my backpack and left. I didn't wait until they were all in bed because it had finally sunk in that no one cared anyway. The only thing that was bothering me was the fact that I was only twelve and, if I was found, the police would simply take me back home again. I went to Holly's and told her that things were getting worse. I didn't go into any detail – perhaps I should have – and I think she just assumed I was being hit even more than I had implied in the past.

She said I could stay in their cellar that night as her parents were going out and they wouldn't be back until late. When they got in, they'd go straight to bed so wouldn't be suspicious of anything. I went straight down and actually managed to sleep quite well that night – it was as if a huge burden had been lifted off my shoulders.

The next morning, Holly came down for me and said I had to go. Her dad was going to be at home all day and she couldn't guarantee he wouldn't come to the cellar. She seemed a bit nervous but I put this down to her not wanting to anger her dad.

'I know where you can go though,' she told me. 'My auntie has a cellar she never uses. I'll give you the address. She's on holiday just now anyway so you can go there without anyone disturbing you. It's always open, there won't be any problems.'

Holly was a life-saver. I hugged her and took the bit of paper with the directions. Hours later, I finally found the place. Just as Holly had said, the cellar was unlocked and I made my way into it. I was a little scared as this time I wasn't with a friend, but I knew I would be willing to do anything to survive and stay away from home.

I spent the rest of the day there. I only had a few tangerines with me which I had brought from home, and I was really cold. When I heard footsteps coming down the stairs, I was relieved. Holly had said her aunt was on holiday so I assumed it must be my friend coming to see me – hopefully with some food.

When she put her head around the door, I was delighted.

'Holly!' I yelled, running over to her.

She didn't smile and I could see she was wary of coming close to me.

'What's wrong?' I asked.

'I'm sorry, Tracy,' she said. 'I'm really sorry.'

Behind her stood her father – and my dad.

'What have you done?' I whispered, trapped in the cellar, with no way of escaping his clutches. 'What have you done?'

'I had to tell,' she said. 'Your dad came round looking for you and mine said I had better tell him everything if I knew what was good for me.' I recognised the hidden threat in that. 'It's only hitting,' she said, dropping her voice. 'You'll get through it. Everyone gets hits by their dad.' She had no idea. No idea at all.

Dad put out his hand for me. I ignored it and climbed the stairs, resigned to going back to my own personal hellhole. When I got out to the street, there were two other men waiting there as well: military police.

'You see, Tracy?' said my dad in a superior voice. 'Do you see how much trouble you cause? Your mum was so worried about you that she had to call the police. You've done so many bad things in the past that this is really going to have terrible consequences for you.' He could hardly keep the smirk off his face, but as I looked at the police officers, I didn't see a threat – I saw a way out.

'I want to talk to them,' I stated.

'What?' said Dad.

'I want to talk to the police.'

His face dropped. 'Well, that'll probably happen. They might want to talk to you. But, for now, let's get you home.'

'No,' I insisted. 'I want to talk to them now.'

One of the officers stepped forward. They had obviously been listening. I'm sure my dad would have thought they would scare me enough simply by being there, that they would know my track record, that there was something troubled in my background.

'Actually, Mr Black, we'd like to speak with Tracy, too,' the officer said.

'Let me get her home, she'll be tired,' he said. His fake concern only alerted me to the fact that he wanted to get me alone to manipulate me again.

'No. We want to talk to her now.'

'I want to talk to you as well,' I said, and walked over to their car, which was clearly marked. I opened the door and got in, while Dad tried to follow.

'I need to talk to you without my dad,' I said quickly to the officer in front.

'We need to have him with you because of your age.'

'No. No, you don't,' I maintained. 'He's the reason I've been doing all of this, starting fires, running away, vandalising things.'

He looked out of the window at my dad standing with the other military policemen. 'What do you mean?'

I closed my eyes and gathered my strength, then said the words which no one had believed at any other time. This was my last chance, I knew that.

'He's been touching me. My dad's been touching me since I was five. I can't go back; I can't take it any more. Please help me.'

And he did.

Someone finally did.

CHAPTER 19

PLAUSIBLE

They didn't let Dad in the car, and I had to wait until another vehicle arrived for him, which followed me to Army headquarters. Nothing was said to me in the car, but the officer I had spoken to had stepped outside before we left and had a quiet word with his colleague, presumably telling him everything. I kept my eyes closed and didn't even look at my father.

When we arrived, I wondered how many people already knew what I had said – *alleged*, I suppose – as I felt everyone was looking at me. That was probably my imagination, but I felt so vulnerable, so naked.

I was told I was being taken to speak to 'the boss'. By this they meant Commanding Officer Stewart, someone I had never met before. It was terrifying to think that my future was in the hands of a man who was a complete stranger to me. I hadn't met many men I could trust, so I had low expectations of this one too.

I sat outside his office for two hours. There was a clock

on the wall and I watched the hands slowly crawl round, wondering what decisions were being taken about me without my input. By this time, I knew it wasn't my imagination which made me think people were looking at me – they definitely were, and I'm sure the story must have spread like wildfire.

By the time I walked into the office, I was shaking.

The CO was a posh man. To me, he sounded like someone off the telly or radio, but he had tremendous warmth to him as well. He was tall and quite thin, with a great gentleness to him.

'I've had a chat with your dad,' he said, 'and he denies it. He denied everything, all of those accusations you made, and told me that you were just saying all of this to cover up getting into trouble.'

I wasn't too surprised by the CO's reaction. There may have been a tiny sliver of hope that he would have believed me, but 'tiny' was the operative word. I thought he would throw me out of the office there and then, but he continued to speak.

'Why did you do those things? Why did you keep getting into trouble?'

'To stop it all, to stop him touching me – and all of that,' I admitted, not having the power of the word 'abuse' to throw at him at that stage.

'How would that stop it?' he asked.

I hadn't actually thought it out that well myself, but the words came to me without any prior working through of it. 'I thought that, if people saw that I was being bad, they'd ask why. No one had ever paid attention to me – not when I was smelly, not when I was covered in bruises. I thought that, maybe, if I started damaging things, property, they might sit up and take notice.'

The commanding officer was quiet for while. 'I see,' he finally responded. 'It worked, didn't it? You have been noticed, Tracy.'

'I just wanted him to stop. I just wanted it all to stop.'

Again, there was a period of silence; then CO Stewart finally said one thing.

'It's plausible.'

That was it.

No more, no less, but in those words came the tiny sliver of hope again.

'There's nothing we can do right now,' he said.

'I'm not going home!'

'I know that. I'm not asking you to, but I've got nowhere really to put you apart from a cell. You'll be safe, Tracy. I'll make sure the door is left open at all times and you only need to ask for whatever you want. There will be a female officer sitting outside all night. Do you think that would be all right?'

It would be more than all right. It would be, hopefully, a turning point.

'Thank you,' I whispered, 'thank you so much.'

He smiled at me, and repeated the words that meant a great deal. 'It's plausible, Tracy; it's plausible.' I know now that he could never have shouted his belief in me or accepted it all instantly, but his reaction made me wonder.

Had there been suspicions about my dad or his friends? Had anyone else made an allegation? I would never know – perhaps CO Stewart was just a good man who put children first. His actions over the next few days would certainly suggest that was a major part of his character.

He said goodbye and wished me well when a female soldier came and escorted me to the cell. I wasn't scared of being in there; I was only scared of going back home. She sat outside the whole time and, although she didn't speak to me, I was reasonably settled for a while.

As time went on, I did my best to not think of what might happen. It was getting late in the day and the sky was darkening, when I heard voices outside and the door opened. It was Commanding Officer Stewart. He asked how I was and checked that I had everything I needed – he was a kind man, but I knew that he was building up to something, as he seemed a little nervous. 'Tracy,' he said, 'I have to tell you that, as a result of what you spoke to me about, I have been asked to ensure that you meet with a doctor.'

That seemed fine to me; I wasn't ill, so the doctor wouldn't have to give me medicine or injections, and I'd tell them just that. When I made these points to CO Stewart, he sat down and spoke gently.

'Actually, Tracy, the doctor will need to examine you for other reasons. We need to know exactly what has happened – we need to know whether there has been any damage.'

There had been plenty of damage, I could tell him that, but I guessed what he was really referring to – this doctor would want to check my body; they would want to look at places I didn't want anyone to look. They wanted to know if I was a liar. It was something I would have to get through because I knew there would be some evidence, some clue – there *had* to be – but I was under no illusions that it would be horrible and yet another invasion of my privacy.

'It would be absolutely fine for you to have your social worker with you,' the CO went on, 'and I'd be more than happy to contact her now and request her presence.'

I snorted. 'She's a waste of space,' I told him. 'She didn't help me when I asked her to, and I don't want anything to do with her.' I felt a little bad being so rude to him, but the very thought of that woman angered me, and her attendance at any medical examination would offer me no comfort at all. To be honest, I was feeling numb and exhausted by this point, and the prospect of the examination itself was just something else for me to get through.

About an hour later, I was taken to a little room along the corridor from the cells in the same building. It seemed the sort of place where basic medical supplies were held, so was probably used for minor injury treatment. For those purposes, it was no doubt fine – but for what I was about to endure, it was cold and charmless. The room was small and drab, and didn't even seem very clinical. It had a sort of musty smell, not one of antiseptic or soap, which is what I might have expected had I given it much thought.

There was a female nurse waiting for me, wearing a white uniform. When I entered the room, she said 'Hello' and asked me to take my clothes off behind a screen so that

I could put on a medical gown. It was huge and white, and looked like a sack on my childish frame. I could hear the nurse moving about, opening and closing doors, as I changed and placed my clothes on a steel-backed chair. She called to me that I should lie down on the examination table and cover myself with the blanket, which was there when I was ready, and then I heard the door open and close. She had gone.

The table was long and thin, rather like a stretcher. It was black and covered in something like leather – as an adult, I know now that there was something missing; there were no stirrups for an internal examination but I didn't realise that at the time.

As I lay there, I tried to find something to focus on. The room was at the far end of the building, so there was no noise to listen out for; no snatched conversations to distract me. There was a small window to the side which looked out onto the woods, but it was very late in the day by then and getting quite dark, so I couldn't be preoccupied by anything there either. The only thing for me to look at, as I waited for the doctor, was an uncovered light bulb in the ceiling. I remember thinking, *if I look at that hard enough, will I go blind?* It was a warning that many parents tell their children about the sun but, for me, I was wishing it was a viable option. I was sick of looking at things, at people, at life.

I got up and sat on a wooden chair while I waited. A few minutes later, the same nurse and a male doctor came in. He was wearing a white coat too.

Plausible

'Hello,' he said. 'I'm Dr Fraser and I'm the medical officer who will be examining you.' He was polite and professional, and explained what he was going to do – but not why. I was told that my heart and pulse would be checked, and that he would *look inside* me. I think I must have looked horrified – which I was – because he said that it wouldn't hurt, that he would be gentle, and that he just needed to make sure everything was all right. While I sat on the chair, he checked my heart and breathing, rattled off the findings to the nurse, then asked me to lie down.

I walked nervously over to the examination table and he followed me as the nurse stayed some distance away. I lay down and he gently pushed my gown up over my hips and placed the blanket over what he had uncovered. The whole experience, from when he checked my heartbeat to when the internal was over, only took about ten minutes – but what really sticks in my mind is the one phrase I heard the doctor say – *her hymen is broken*. The words never really meant anything to me that day, but I knew from the way he said them – a low voice, assertive, determined – that this was important. It wasn't until I was a couple of years older and studying biology at school that the meaning of the statement became apparent and I understood that this physical fact had actually given them some objective, incontrovertible evidence to back up my claims.

On that day when I was in the examination room, my only thought when he said it, was whether it meant my Dad had broken me in some way. My mind raced from wondering whether it had happened because of his attacks, or

197

because I had been bad by telling of our secret. I didn't know what 'hymen' meant but it was 'broken', which was registering loud and clear.

Dr Fraser said he was finished and that I should get dressed quickly because it was getting cold. As he got ready to leave, he smiled and asked if I was all right – I nodded as he walked out. The nurse said very little but took me back to my cell when I was dressed; it was never spoken of again by anyone. I was never told if my parents knew of the findings or if it was discussed with them at all. The embarrassment I felt when it was all taking place was acute, but I tried to remove myself from the experience – something I had plenty of practice with – and just took some comfort from the fact that at least something was finally being done.

In the cell, I lay down on the narrow bed and tried to sleep. I was still exhausted, but any rest I managed was fitful. Time did pass however, and, sometime in the early hours, a soldier put his head around the door and asked, 'Are you awake?' I sat up on the narrow bed, rubbing my eyes. 'Not speaking?' he commented. 'Get your head into this,' he said, tossing me a book. 'It might teach you fucking something.' The woman outside said nothing, she did nothing, didn't even flinch. I can't even remember what it was called, but it was a story about a girl who had been abused by her stepfather and it was by Harold Robbins. The story told of how she killed him and went on to become a prostitute. I only read so much and left it there when I was called out. I should have taken it to the CO and told him what that man had given me. It went through my mind that he was probably one of them, one of the paedophile ring I now had no doubt my dad was part of.

It also made me realise that they must have all known what I was there for, because the woman who was sitting outside my cell seemed to be on his side. He had looked at me as if I was dirt and had thrown me something she hadn't even checked, so presumably she was of the mind that a nasty little girl had made ludicrous allegations about her 'hero' father, one of her colleagues. While I was there, most of the other guards were distant, but fine, apart from him.

After breakfast, I was told that CO Stewart wanted to see me again in his office. It felt as if my heart was going to beat out of my chest. My tummy was in knots and I was just so worried that the relative safety I had been offered since I had last met with him would be snatched away again. I was taken along the corridor from the cell and all I could think about was whether the CO had changed his mind – would he still be so kind today, or would he shout at me and say he didn't believe a word?

I was so wrapped up in my own thoughts that I wasn't really paying attention to where we were. Before I knew it, we were outside the CO's office – and we weren't alone. Sitting there, on hard, plastic seats, were my parents. They were there to take me back to my own private hell, I was sure of it. But this time would be worse, because this time I had committed the cardinal sin – I had told someone.

Mum couldn't even raise her eyes to look at me. After all this time, after all the time she had failed to love me, failed to save me, there was still a part of me which remained an innocent child desperate for her mummy. If only she had rushed to me, held me in her arms and said everything would be all right. If only I had seen some shred of affection from her, I would have thought it was all worth it.

Unsurprisingly, there was nothing.

She kept staring at the floor, her face hard.

I'd rather my father had been doing that, but he chose to look me in the face, hatred written all over him. He fixed me with his eyes and I knew then he would never admit to anything. From what I could tell, he had no remorse. He was a paedophile who had raped and abused his own daughter for years, and would have happily had many more men do the same – I was as likely to get an apology from him as I was to get a cuddle from my mum.

I thought I heard him call me names as I went into the CO's office – *bitch, whore, slut, prostitute* – but perhaps they were just echoes of the years gone by when those were the only words he ever used for me.

I was shaking as I stood before CO Stewart again. I had run the gauntlet – was I now to be returned to the people outside that door who seemed to hate me so much?

'Please sit down, Tracy,' he said, smiling kindly as soon as I went into his room. 'Did you sleep well? Did you have everything you needed?' I nodded because, really, I wanted him to like me, to think I was no bother, and to believe I was a trustworthy girl who deserved his help. 'I've given this a great deal of thought and, under the circumstances, you have two choices – you can go back home, or never go back home again.'

I could hardly believe it.

'You mean it? I can choose to never go back there? Ever?'

'Yes. If that's what you want. Is that what you want?'

'Yes! Yes, of course it is!' I responded.

He allowed himself to smile at my obvious happiness. 'You will have to go back for your things but you won't be alone.'

I could do that – but what about long term, I wondered?

'And school?' I asked. 'What will happen about school?'

'It's all taken care of,' he assured me. 'If you never want to go back there again, it's all taken care of.'

'But where will I go? Won't I have to live at home so that I can go to school?'

'I've arranged for you to go to a different school.'

I still didn't comprehend what was going on. No matter which local school I went to, surely I would still be living with my parents, with my dad?

'Which school?' I pushed.

'You'll be going to a British Army boarding school here in Germany. There's nothing to worry about, it's all been sorted.'

It seemed as if everything had indeed already been decided. I felt that CO Stewart knew which option I'd go for, and that he had made sure everything was in place – whatever it was going to be – by the time I went into his office that morning. He suggested I go back to the cell and try to sleep for a few hours as I had an emotionally draining time ahead of me. 'When you wake up, you'll be able to go back home for everything you need. Your mum has ... well, she's gone away for the day, and there will be a military police officer with you when you leave here.'

'She's out there, though,' I said. 'Mum's out there.'

'No,' he replied. 'She won't be there when you leave this room. I can assure you of that.'

There was such strength to this man, and I'll never forget him. When he spoke, I believed him, and when I wondered if he might be able to wave a magic wand and sort things for me, I actually felt as if he could. I had no idea what discussions, or indeed arguments or threats, had gone on in the background, but CO Stewart had obviously been working hard during the night and I would do anything he suggested.

As I went to leave the room, he called my attention. 'Tracy – I'm sorry, but your father will have to be there when you return home. Legally, he is still your guardian and, in the absence of your mother, he will have to supervise things. As I've said though, you will never be alone with him – there will be a policeman there with you at all times. Everything is in place for you. I wish you the best.'

My heart sank at the thought of being anywhere near my father, even for a little while and even under the protection of the military police. What if the person charged with looking after me was like him? What if they thought I was a liar and left me alone with him? I had no idea what he would do – I felt I had only seen some of what he was capable of, and it was bad enough. I felt angry that my mum had removed herself from the situation yet again. I guess it was a hard habit for her to break; it's what she had been doing for years. I could only assume she had been told what was happening and didn't want to be anywhere near me, but her selfishness was leaving me vulnerable yet again and placing me in direct contact with the very man I had accused and who I never wanted to be near again in my life.

I went home and packed in a daze. I was so sure that Dad would shout at me, rant and try to find a way to get at me, to hit me and do something awful. He didn't even come out of the living room. Gary wasn't there. Mum wasn't there. None of my friends were playing in the street. It was as if this was the last chapter of a story which was now coming to a close and all the major players, except me and my dad, had simply walked away. I was stunned that Dad just accepted it, but so relieved.

It only took me about five minutes to get my things.

I walked out of my room for the last time and said I was ready to leave. I closed the door behind me in silence and walked out of the house which had been my prison.

There were no fanfares or fireworks. There was no shouting or crying.

I just walked.

I just walked out.

I felt the most tremendous gratitude to the man who had made all of this possible. CO Stewart was so sympathetic and understanding. I never felt he doubted me or put any blame on me. He fixed everything and knew I needed to be taken away. He had time for me and just seemed to work it all out instantly. I don't know how he managed to make things work the way they did that day, but I will never forget him. I don't know what really happened, but sometimes I've wondered if, in exchange for allowing me to go, my father was told no charges would be pressed and he took the escape route being offered.

I went back to headquarters with two bags, which contained everything I owned. The next day I would start my new life.

It had been a long time coming.

CHAPTER 20

MY NEW HOME

Boarding school was a totally different world for me. I know that in recent years lots of people have said the whole boarding school experience is a world away from the *Harry Potter* stories, and that it's a hard life with children left to fend for themselves in quite a harsh environment – there were certainly no witches or wizards at mine, but it was still a wonderful place for me to be. It was safe and that alone was priceless. I could even say that was magical in itself.

For a start, there was a uniform. I still had memories of those years when I was in charge of my own laundry and everything I owned stank of damp and neglect. Years of being called 'stinky' – and worse – were forgotten when I put on my smart new blazer and skirt. The blazers came in a choice of burgundy or black, and I went for the former as it was more colourful, more of an indication that this was a new start for me. The school tie was burgundy and white to match, and we wore grey or burgundy jumpers with grey or black skirts. It was all new. Nothing was passed down or second-hand and I pressed every single item to my nose time after time, just to wallow in the smell of cleanliness.

I didn't have the pleasure or excitement of shopping for my uniform. In fact, up until the last minute, I didn't even know for sure I was going to have one at all. The day after I arrived, Matron sent a message to the dorm that she wanted to see me. As I walked down the steps to her office, I was shaking with nerves – what if she told me it was all a terrible mistake? What if Dad had refused permission for me to attend, or the commanding officer had decided I was a liar? What if I had to go back? I started making tentative escape plans because I knew there was absolutely no way I could bear returning to that house, to *him*. I had no money, no friends or family to go to, but I couldn't even contemplate voluntarily returning to my abuser and the promise of more attacks on me.

I was still suspicious of people, still wary of anything that looked like it might be an escape route – especially now I feared it was all going to be snatched away. As a result, when I walked in and Matron warmly welcomed me with a smile as she said, 'Hello, Tracy, how nice to see you,' I was still waiting for the worst.

'Do sit down,' she said, indicating a soft chair in the corner. I did as I was told, and she walked towards me carrying a pile of clothes. She looked rather embarrassed. 'Here is your uniform, dear – I'm very sorry but ... your father was rather busy and couldn't wait to hand it over personally or see you.'

There was no need for her to apologise. I was delighted.

206

Three wonderful things had happened in the space of a few seconds – I was now sure I was being allowed to stay; I was being provided with a brand-new uniform; and, best of all, I didn't have to see my dad. There was no doubt in my mind that Matron was being diplomatic and that Dad hadn't wanted to see me in front of an audience, but, given that I didn't want to see him either, this wasn't a source of disappointment.

'I'm sorry, Tracy,' Matron commiserated. I felt a little guilty I couldn't put her mind at ease and tell her she had nothing to be sorry for, but I couldn't do that without opening up a whole can of worms.

I thanked her and rushed back to the dorm, smelling the new clothes and grinning uncontrollably. Two of every item nestled in my arms, and everything was of the best quality. I wondered then, as I do now, who really paid for it all – it seems extremely unlikely my father would fork out, so I considered the likelihood that perhaps, once again, the Army had come to my rescue.

The school consisted of seven different houses, each holding about one hundred girls. All of them, as well as the teaching and administration offices, were held within very long buildings. Some were red-brick, some were whitewash, and each was three or four floors high, with one in front of the other. Five minutes away was the boys' boarding school, and their version had exactly the same layout. The gate entrance was usually manned, but that didn't stop fraternisation between the schools – there is nothing as determined as a teenager who is told not to do something! When I eventually did meet some of the boy pupils, I had to go along with the notion they perpetuated that the schools were awful places. They called them Stalag Compound X or whatever – I called mine Heaven.

It was like being back in the Army base in some ways as each school was similar to a little village. There were playing fields and a netball court, there was a dining room and assembly hall, there was a swimming pool, a sick bay and lots of classrooms. Every place holds its own memories for me – but all of them are good. The discipline and restrictions of boarding school life held no horrors for me, for I had a freedom within those rules I had never had before, a freedom from being nothing more than a plaything for my sick father. What did it matter to me that I had homework and exams? I soon found out that I had a brain. What did it matter that I wasn't allowed out except under strict directions and promises? I was safe in school and on school grounds, so didn't particularly want to go anywhere else.

Each of the houses had a matron of their own, and the girls used to say they were worse than mothers. This, again, was alien to me – my mum hadn't exactly been the traditional type, and what I really wanted was what these matrons wanted to provide, namely safety and security. There were times when I 'talked the talk' with the other girls who liked to moan about the restrictions placed on them, but, to be honest, I loved the way in which I was looked after. I had no inclination to run about with boys or have sex on the sly, I just wanted to keep away from my dad.

My matron was called Frau Schneider, a small, rather

plump woman, with the voice of a docker! When she shouted, everybody listened, but she also had a true kindness to her. She used to breed and show Hungarian Puli dogs, the fancy types whose fur grows like dreadlocks. Everyone loved her and her dogs. Frau Schneider had ten of them, and she would regale us with tales of their adventures and characters as well as keeping two at the school. One of them, Kaiser, was enormous, a black Puli with huge hanging dreadlocks all over his legs and tail. I don't remember why, but one day, some girls, including me, decided we'd try and brush those dreads out. That was a disaster – Frau Schneider had spent a fortune on Kaiser, and was very proud of his looks, with the 'dreads' being a very distinct look for the breed. She went ballistic when she found we had turned him to frizz, but never found out who was responsible. The tuck shop visit that day was suspended for all girls in my house – if you ever read this, Frau Schneider, my apologies ... but Kaiser did seem to enjoy the attention!

Dorms usually held four to six girls – there were four in mine, including myself – and they were pretty spacious. Ours had two metal-framed bunk beds and a wardrobe sectioned into four spaces. Each girl had her own chest of drawers. There was a desk to share and a lockable cupboard each. The cupboard was for the things we thought were most important to us – and that usually meant food, so they tended to be full of coffee, sugar, biscuits and sweets. I kept my cigarettes there too. The windows were framed by heavy curtains and there was an overall feeling of everything necessary being provided, with no luxuries. It was better than anything I'd ever had.

If dorms were messy or beds unmade, the house matron would strip the beds and empty the drawers into the middle of the floor. Each house also had a housemistress and a house prefect; the housemistress was usually a teacher and the prefect was a sixth-former. As well as these, each floor had its own monitor, so there were plenty of people to keep us in check. Every new boarder was matched up with a senior girl for a week or two until they got used to the place. They showed you where to go – gym, dinner hall, classrooms, assembly – and made sure you knew all the rules and regulations. I guess, in some ways, it was like a children's version of the Army and, because of that, I fitted in quite well.

Just as it had been at all of the Army schools, we were taught in English not German – German language was an option though and, even now, I'm quite fluent. Every morning we would have a roll call. All of us lined up outside our dorm and names were called out. This was to ensure none of us had run away during the night – that never happened that I knew of, although there were plenty of late-night excursions the staff were unaware of. They did try to keep tabs on us and sometimes there would be roll call in the wee small hours if they suspected something. However, while there were plenty of girls who knew just how to sneak out to the boys' school, they always seemed to know when a middle-of-the-night roll call was being mooted, so avoided those times. They were communication and spying experts the Army would have been proud of – maybe it was in their genes!

After roll call, mail was handed out. Needless to say, I never received any but always hoped Mum would write one day. She never did. Our pocket money, usually ten Deutschmarks, would come from the matron but sometimes a girl might get extra from her parents when opening her mail.

The other three girls in my dorm were very different from each other, and they were all there for very different reasons to me as well. I remember them so well, as they were the first close group I had ever belonged to. I recall the way they dressed, the things they liked, the passions they had, clearer than my own, because they were just normal girls going through their teenage years with no baggage.

Jodie was the daughter of an RSM (a Regimental Sergeant Major). The official reason for her being there was that there was no school where she lived. I always suspected her parents didn't know quite what to do with her and were delighted to get a rest. Jodie was the outrageous one. She was sporty and loud, she joked a lot and was always up for a laugh. She was constantly getting caught smoking and the teachers frequently disciplined her for swearing, which would put most of her father's Army colleagues to shame. Jodie was very boyish, she had short hair and preferred trousers, mostly opting for 'skinners'. She would often wear Doc Marten boots and was the least interested in looking girlish. One of the other girls in the dorm used to say she brought shame on our room because of the way she dressed, and she was only half-joking. Her

words, however, seemed to make Jodie even more determined to keep to her own fashion style.

Kate was at boarding school because her parents were on
a posting to Singapore. She was the tallest of our group.
She had long black hair and freckles all over her face (which
she hated). Kate was also very sporty and participated in all
the after-school sports, being especially good at hockey and
netball. She was a sensible dresser who had a penchant for
long flared skirts and a twinset, clothes which were very
grown-up really but suited her mature character. She was
the mother figure in our group as she constantly worried
about the other girls, especially if there was any bullying.
She was concerned about every other girl, not just those of
us in our dorm. On one occasion, a new pupil was being bullied by someone from another house completely. It was Kate
who warned the older girl that she would have to deal with
all of us if the bullying continued. She seemed to have a
radar for it. Although I never saw her being bullied herself,
she often alluded to being the victim of it when she was
much younger, and I guess that's what made her such a
fighter for other younger, weaker pupils who were at the
mercy of the established thugs who ruin any school. Kate
had brought a small record player with her, which was a
delight for all of us. It was the mid 1970s, and music seemed
as important to teenagers as breathing – perhaps fewer
things have changed than we realise.

Amy was a pretty girl of slight build with dark-brown
hair cut into pageboy style. She was the eldest in our room
and very popular throughout the school. Amy was an only

child, quite a flirtatious girl, fun-loving and daring, yet also sensible, never overstepping the mark. Her father was high-ranking in the Army and the family was always on the move. At the odd school disco she would keep the boys interested, dancing and flirting with them during the evening, but she never left with anyone in all the time I knew her. Amy had very particular clothes preferences. She'd never be seen in jeans other than Levi's, and she loved pretty flowery blouses.

The atmosphere in the dorm was a happy, relaxed one – even when Frau Schneider was on the warpath, we all pulled together and had a laugh. We would spend hours talking about music, playing draughts and Twister. The latter was our favourite board game of all, even if it did usually result in a ticking off from Matron because of the hilarity it caused as we mangled ourselves into ever more contorted shapes.

These were new and welcome experiences for me. I had friends who knew nothing of my history – at that point. I had food and clean clothes and safety. The only thing I found uncomfortable to begin with was the constant chattering about boys. How could I, at that age and with my background, fall into the easy gossiping of my new friends? For them, falling in love was something which hinted promise and excitement. Sex would come eventually and it would be part of the natural order, at the right time and in the right context. I managed to join in with the breathless wondering about which boys were good-looking and what they would be like as boyfriends, but there was always a part of me which wondered what Kate, Jodie and Amy would think if I told them the truth. It played on my mind a lot during those early days – what would they call me if they knew I'd already had sex? What would they really feel about me if they knew I had let my dad do all those things to me? Would they still be my friends, or would they turn into enemies, calling me names and making me feel so much less than them?

I kept it all to myself, but that would change.

For the time being, this was my new life and I revelled in it.

CHAPTER 21

A SENSE OF NORMALITY

This four-year period was an island of peace and security in my young life. After a while, I would wake up in the morning without my stomach in knots; I was finally allowing myself to believe I was going to be allowed to stay and I could look to the future. My parents didn't keep in touch and never visited. I'd be lying if I said that didn't hurt because there was always a small, unrealistic, part of me which hoped they would change – that, one day, Dad would turn up in floods of tears to apologise for everything he'd done to me over the years and come up with some miraculous excuse for the abuse. This excuse was one which, no matter how hard I tried, I could never think of, which isn't surprising – how could you ever excuse what he did? In my daydreams, it would all be sorted. I would forget the pain and the horror, and he would turn into the dad I'd always wanted. In this Disney version of my life, my mum was also part of the turnaround. She'd roll up to school, draw me into her arms and hug me as we both marvelled at our love for each other.

Fat chance.

They never even wrote.

The upside was that, without Dad poisoning my life and Mum withholding all love, I had the chance to make a new world for myself. Amy, Jodie and Kate were the members of my new family. It was my chance to be young – at last. On one occasion, we were lying back on pillows from our beds in the dorm. Flicking through magazines Kate had been sent, I saw a picture which made me drool with jealously. In it, the model had extraordinarily huge Afro hair, the style which was becoming so fashionable , no matter the race or genetic make-up of the wearer. In fact, during that time, there was an explosion of the hairdo, which paid no heed at all to the appropriateness of who was sporting it – strange times!

As we sat there looking at the glossy pictures, I couldn't help but say, 'I wish my hair was like that.' The words were hardly out of my mouth before Jodie shot back, 'Get the perming stuff, Tracy, and I'll do it for you.' The plans were made immediately. Jodie, of course, had absolutely no hair-dressing experience, but we all got carried away, and that little detail seemed unimportant. The next time we went into town, I collected everything from the local chemist. Weeks of planning were now going to come to fruition and all I could think of was the wonderful new hair I would be sporting.

We all rushed back to the dorm with the paper bag full of hairdressing requirements. Amy and Kate sat down to watch, while Jodie waltzed around like Vidal Sassoon. I sat there with a towel around my shoulders while she fumbled around with the perming lotion – which I thought would strip the nose lining from all of us before the afternoon was over – and squirted it all over my head. The curlers were wound tightly around my hair and the lotion was dripping from them. I could feel it burning and my eyes wouldn't stop streaming. However, youthful optimism was stronger than the evidence, and we all looked forward to my marvellous new Afro.

To be fair, when the curlers and papers were taken out, it wasn't too bad. Our excitement over having had something to plan and execute – and the relief that I wasn't bald – made me think I looked fantastic. Maybe I did – for about two days. As time went on, my hair got fluffier and fluffier. If it got wet in the shower or a few raindrops hit it, it seemed to expand in seconds. By the end of a week, I looked like a maniacal lion. My hair was about ten times the size it should have been, and it seemed to need shearing rather than hair products. Which is exactly what happened – after many comments from the other girls and lots of 'suggestions' from Frau Schneider, I traipsed to the town hairdresser, only two weeks after I had gloried in my gorgeous Afro. It was all sheared off and I went back to normal hair. I was rather relieved actually.

As I was gaining more confidence in my new life, my past was something I tried not to think about. It wasn't that I had forgotten those awful years since I was five – how could I ever forget that? – but I was trying to forget to remember, if that makes sense. Every time a feeling or a thought popped up, I would try my best to squash it back down. I didn't *want* to think, I didn't *want* to remember. What I really needed was to become as ordinary as possible and, although the very thought terrified me, that involved being interested in boys.

I looked on it as playing a part in a school play. I would just have to *act* a different Tracy. Jodie was the one who was really keen on getting me to join in her excursions to the boys' school, but I preferred it when Amy was involved – when she ventured out on expeditions to the other school, she realised it was only for fun and no other reason. Some girls, including Jodie, would drink bottles of beer or Apfelkorn before venturing out; on these occasions, Amy made sure she didn't go with her and I liked the sense she brought to the trips. Alongside some other girls from a different house, we would sneak out and go across enemy lines. All we would do when we got there was sit and smoke, having a chat, usually about music and school – but each time it felt as if I was taking my life in my hands. What would have happened if we had got caught? Some of the other girls were found out, and they had their privileges suspended for a week or more. To me, the worse thing was that their parents were told too. I would break out in a cold sweat just thinking about it – I needed to create an ordinary, normal version of myself, but if teachers knew I had been visiting boys, would they tell my parents? Would they tell the CO who had done so much to help me? This was what really scared me. If CO Stewart heard such tales, what would he think? I thought I knew – I was sure it would make him rue the day he had believed me; he would think I was a liar, a slut who chased after boys, a manipulative girl who didn't deserve to be at boarding school.

What if he took me away?

If I was caught and my parents were told, it would surely mean no one would ever believe me if I did ever find the courage again to say what Dad had been doing to me. He would be the one with all the power again – his daughter would be proved to be a two-faced boy-mad liar, and people would never believe what I alleged.

I had only been across to the boys' boarding school a few times, but I stopped doing even that and just listened to what the other girls were doing. Usually these escapades were for a dare. The girls would make a hole in the fence and try to cover it with bushes. Matron continually checked the fence behind our house, which was seven feet high and made of metal with barbed wire along the top. Night watchmen with dogs patrolled the perimeter and it felt like Colditz in the dead of night – hardly worth risking for a natter with a couple of spotty lads, and certainly not worth it for me as I had so much to lose.

I met a lot of really nice kids at that school, and even bumped into one from my Rinteln days. Diana Hayes was a 'day bug' – this was the name for pupils who didn't lodge and who only came to the school for the day. Diana's father was a captain and I was delighted to see her as we had been to the same primary and secondary schools as each other for a while. It was even easier to get on with Diana because, as her father was so much higher up in the regiment than my dad, they had never socialised, so I was comforted that my two worlds could be keep distinct from each other.

There were a lot of day bugs at the school, usually children who lived locally in areas such as Soest and Werl. They were tolerated by most boarders rather than warmly welcomed, and the two groups tended to keep themselves to themselves. Even in the classrooms, boarders would sit with boarders and day pupils with day pupils. I also met one of the boys I had fought with previously – Olly Wilson. What a difference a year had made – not only did he seem human at school, we actually managed to get on!

During the week and during normal activities, I found it quite easy to keep my new facade in place. I was Normal Tracy. When letters came, and there was nothing for me, I acted as if I didn't care. When parents sent parcels and extra pocket money, and I was given things by friends because I had nothing of my own, I was blasé. It took a few months before the other girls noticed there was never anything for me. They were starting to get excited about going home for the Christmas holidays. This wasn't something I could join in with. I was dreading going back and couldn't imagine being allowed to leave home again once the festive season was over. What if Dad kept me at home and never allowed me out again? The abuse would surely restart and be even worse, if possible, now I had revealed all to CO Stewart.

One evening, Jodie asked the question I had been dreading. As we sat around the table eating supper, she said the words I didn't want to hear. 'Why do your parents never write to you, Tracy?'

A Sense of Normality

At that point, I wished I'd lied when I arrived at boarding school. If only I had said they were dead, that I was an orphan, it would have been easier. As it was, I had given some story about my dad getting lots of different postings and my parents wanting me to have some continuity with my education. I should have known that lie would be found out because it made them seem caring and concerned about me, which was at odds with them never writing or sending parcels.

'Don't know,' I muttered, but she wouldn't let it drop.

'They never send you parcels either, do they?' she continued. 'Why's that?'

'No idea – maybe they don't know the address,' I half-joked, praying she would change the subject.

'I think it's odd,' she went on.

'Just leave it,' said Kate. She was always the one concerned about the feelings of others and I'm sure she could see I was uncomfortable.

'Never mind – you'll feel even more excited about going home for Christmas then, won't you?' finished Jodie. 'You've heard nothing from them since you got here and had no parcels, so they must be planning a brilliant homecoming for you.'

I had been trying not to think about it. As the Christmas decorations went up throughout the school and the girls started talking about the holidays, I had pushed it all to the back of my mind. Matron had said nothing, and I'd had no clues from home, so I didn't know when they'd be coming for me or what would be happening.

Throughout that evening, it was as if Jodie had broken down the carefully constructed barriers I had erected. I had done so well to not face up to what scared me so much, but now she had said it out loud, I had to address the fact that I would be going home soon, and there was no way I could avoid it. For the rest of the night, as we got ready for classes the next day, I felt as if I was totally disconnected from my dorm mates. They were talking, but I could barely hear them. They were trying to engage me in conversation, but I couldn't join in their banter with such a dark cloud hanging over me.

I hardly slept that night. The fear I felt about returning to my dad's care was physical as well as emotional. My stomach was aching and I felt so sick. I ate nothing for breakfast and couldn't concentrate throughout my English class. My temperature was all over the place, hot one minute, freezing cold the next. When class ended, I ran to the toilets before going on to my next lesson. I barely got into the cubicle before I started vomiting. There was little in my tummy as I hadn't been able to eat since Jodie had asked about my Christmas plans and I was very sore very quickly, as I brought up bile.

Throughout that morning, I was sick between every class and I went through the hours in a daze. By early evening, I was in a terrible state. I went down to dinner with the girls, none of whom knew I had been sick all day, and sat at the table, wondering how I would hide the fact I couldn't eat.

I needn't have worried – I wouldn't be there for long.

A Sense of Normality

As I sat, trying to look as if I was listening to Amy and Kate's chatter, I felt faint. I could hear Jodie say, as if from a long way away, 'What's wrong, Tracy? What's wrong?' and then nothing. The next thing I knew, I was in the sick bay.

Frau Schneider was standing over me, looking terribly concerned.

'Tracy? Tracy?' How are you?' she asked.

'Fine, I think – what happened?'

'You collapsed, dear – have you not been eating? Have you been feeling unwell for long? Your friends are awfully worried about you – they're all waiting outside.'

Her kindly face comforted me enormously but I had one thing to ask. 'Frau Schneider – what will be happening to me at Christmas? Is ... is my father coming for me?' I whispered.

I have no idea how much that woman knew, how much she had been told, but as she sat down on the bed and clasped my hand, I suddenly felt as if she had given me a wonderful gift. 'You won't be going home for Christmas, my dear,' she said. 'We're very lucky to have you staying here with us. It's all been ... organised.'

She said nothing more. With a warm squeeze of my hand, she tucked me in and left the room to update my friends on my progress. I clasped my stomach, racked with pain from the vomiting I had suffered earlier that morning. My head was bursting with a hundred thoughts, my heart breaking with a thousand emotions – but, despite all this, the one thing I clung to was the most important thing of all. I was safe. Absolutely, perfectly safe.

It was such a simple thing, a state of mind and body which so many people take for granted, but the twelve-year-old me knew without doubt it was the most precious way to be. For years, I had been abused. For years, I had been prey to the perversions of my father. For years, I had been a plaything for his friends. For years I had been passed between one man and another, men who were well thought of, men who were regarded as heroes – men who found their pleasure in raping and abusing a little girl.

Now, as I lay in the sick bay of the boarding school which had only recently become my refuge, I finally realised it was all over. No longer would I be the pawn of these animals who ignored my cries, ignored my pain. I was alone – apart from the nurse who watched over me – but I was happy. It was time to take charge of my own life. It was time to stop crying in the dark, time to stop taking the blame for the crimes committed against me.

As I lay there that night, I felt at peace.

Things were getting better.

CHAPTER 22

SECRETS

However, there was a school disco to get through first. Just before the Christmas break the hall was transformed into something resembling a teacher's vision of what young people would like – needless to say, like youngsters throughout history, we were damning of the efforts and thought it was all embarrassingly lame. That didn't mean to say most girls had given up their hopes of bagging a boyfriend for the night. For me, I couldn't think of anything I would like less. There were actually two school discos a year, but this would be my first one. I didn't feel comfortable at all when the night arrived. I never really had any interest in boys while I was there and was not looking for a boyfriend at all. I'd paid little attention to what I was wearing and, thankfully, got no boys coming over to me at all, but I also felt left out – most girls had siblings there too so they always had someone to talk to. Still, I held on to the happiness I felt that I would be staying at school for the holidays – I could get through any amount of social embarrassment knowing I had that in my hand.

Before every school disco, the other three girls would practise their dancing in the dorm, each of them choosing their favourite music to move around to. I was more than happy to join in with that, because I loved music, and the dancing part was something which just brought us all closer together as we had such fun doing it.

As with our dress sense, our musical tastes were different. Amy and Kate were keen on David Essex and Rod Stewart. Like most of the girls at school, they also went through a phase of adoring the Bay City Rollers – at one point, the whole school roll seemed to be wearing tartan and I was told on many occasions how lucky I was to be Scottish, even though I'd barely stayed there for any length of time. I was even asked by plenty of girls if I was related to any of the band – being Scottish was enough apparently!

Jodie loved to play one Black Sabbath album just to annoy us all – I'm pretty sure she hated it herself but, like her commitment to skinners and DMs, she got more pleasure out of digging her heels in than from wearing or listening to things she actively liked! Normally she would listen to lighter stuff, such as Status Quo, but we danced along to anything given half a chance. As the record player belonged to Kate, she was the one who got to dictate when it could be used. She organised how long we could listen to it for, and it tended to be half an hour each at the weekends, and sometimes during the week on special occasions.

Life was quite strict, but that didn't bother me; the rules were all for our own good, and they were rarely anything other than normal school regulations. When I stayed at school that Christmas, it was to be the first of a number of holidays I spent there, and they all had the same format. Those who were left behind would watch the other girls getting picked up by their parents or catching the school bus to take them home. The majority of those who remained were there because their parents were still on overseas postings. Those who went away were always so excited at being with their parents again. I felt saddened in a way when I saw them because I wished I could feel that excitement at going home, and there was always the realisation that it would never happen. I consoled myself with the knowledge that, if I did go home, it would be horrible – it hadn't transformed into a fairy-tale life, it would still be hell.

Matron celebrated Christmas with the girls who were left behind. We had to put our shoes or slippers outside the dormitory door. If we had been good we would get sweets in them but if we had been bad we were given sticks, a German tradition. Most of the time we all got a mixture of sweets and sticks, with just enough balance the right way! There was carol singing at the end of our corridor with lights all around, and Matron would light candles for us. It was really warm and caring – I had to be careful not to seem too happy, because all the other girls had a sadness about them due to being apart from their loving families. I couldn't look too delighted at the fact that these were the happiest Christmas memories of my life.

The year after that, I also stayed in the school for the summer holidays. We were given the option to go home with friends if family trips weren't feasible, but I didn't push for this, largely because I feared no one would want me. As always, I preferred not to take the risk of feeling bad, so I opted to get in first and made it clear I had no wish to be with anyone else and would relish some time on my own. One summer, Kate was there for the whole time and that was great. The staff and teachers would take us out on bus trips to places like the Sauerland, a big country park with lakes where we would have picnics and barbecues. There was swimming and fun all summer, and by the next year I was confident enough to believe in the friends I had made. I was delighted when my friend Diana, the one I had known in Rinteln, asked me to stay with her family. I ended up spending a lot of time there, and it was wonderful to see a family that loved each other and who knew how to spend time together. Her parents would take us out a lot – to the cinema, to a theme park that was close by, and on shopping trips.

I loved those trips, and I really appreciated the time I spent with the Hayes family. At times, I pretended to be part of it, dissociating myself from my own horrible experiences of family life and revelling in the ordinariness of it. Diana's parents knew I had been in trouble before and yet they never commented on it; their only worry was that a young girl was left alone at boarding school during the holidays. By this time, my story about my dad always being trans-ferred at short notice was wearing thin, and I also worried that Diana's father might know him, so I used a bit of the truth and started telling people that my mum didn't keep well and was often in hospital, which made it best for me to stay put at school. I have no idea whether they bought that explanation or perhaps wondered if there was more to it than I let on, but I suspected they were just too nice to say anything.

One Christmas time when I was staying with them, Diana told her parents how I never got any presents from my mum and dad at any time of the year and that they never sent parcels to school for me. Mrs Hayes gently told her to not say such things and distracted her attention. The next day there was a pile of gifts for me. The Hayes had gone out and bought me loads of stuff, from make-up to a record I really liked (I remember even to this day it was 'Just Call Me Angel of the Morning'), from a selection box to clothes. Mrs Hayes had even bought me a cherry lip gloss which I coveted hugely, and which was all the rage. It was one of the loveliest things anyone had ever done for me, and it meant even more because they didn't make a song and dance about it. As a child, the little things could have such an effect on me and as a grown-up I have tried to remember that; you never know what a child is going through at home, and simple acts of kindness can make their lives more bearable.

Those Christmas holidays, discos, excursions to the boys' school and days out in Germany formed the backdrop of the next four years of my life. In the middle of it all were the normal things of music, fashion, make-up and friendships, and I felt happier than I ever had before. The lack of contact with my parents had been the norm for such a while, I could almost allow myself to relax and believe they would leave me alone permanently. Of course, I wanted love, but I didn't want it on their terms.

By the time I had been at boarding school for two years, I realised there were more people like me than I had first imagined, both at my school and the one for boys. The majority of kids were there because there was no school for British kids near to where they were living, and there were others whose parents were abroad on long placements. However, there were also others who, like me, had been sent there because they didn't function well within mainstream schools, for whatever reason – usually it was because of truancy and getting into trouble, but my own experiences had led me to realise these activities were often a smokescreen for other, darker problems.

After a while, I started to become inquisitive about why other kids were there – looking back, I think in some ways I was hoping to find someone like me. While I had previously suspected that some children were abused – such as my friend in Northern Ireland, although I never had any evidence of that happening – I had never discussed my own abuse with another youngster. As I became more and more 'normal', I was curious to know how many of us there were. Was there a whole anonymous group of abused children who never knew that others were there because we were all so used to silence and secrecy? The thoughts would go around my head whenever a new pupil arrived – why were they here? What had they done? What had been done to them? Even with friends who seemed to have straightforward family lives, I often wondered. I, of all people, knew what went on behind closed doors. The longer I was away from my dysfunctional family, the more I wondered about others.

David was the son of a private and was in his first year at school with us, so he must have been about twelve when I first met him. He had a younger brother who still stayed with their parents. A few weeks after he arrived, I met him for the first time when some of the girls escaped to the boys' school one weekend. By this time, we knew the boys pretty well and, although some girls had boyfriends, we mostly had a laugh and sometimes a drink with them. David got into the older boys' group very quickly, so I wondered about him. One night, I gathered the courage to ask why he was at boarding school. I tried to phrase the question in a way which would allow him to suspect the true meaning of what I was asking.

'Why are you really here?' I queried.

He looked at me as if I was mad.

'Because I'm a right little shit,' he said.

'Do you want to talk about it?' I asked.

He continued to look at me as if I was the daftest thing he had seen since his arrival and then walked away. 'Talk about *what* exactly?' I heard him say.

The thing was, I didn't know what to ask or what I wanted to hear. Abused children are so used to being told one thing and hearing another that communication can be hard. Black can mean white, night can mean day, and sometimes nothing makes sense. I'd been told that I loved being abused. I'd been told that I enjoyed being raped. I'd been told that I encouraged my dad to violate me. I'd been told that when I allowed all of this to happen, I was a good girl.

Was it any wonder I sometimes felt as if I didn't know the rules by which everyone else lived?

I wasn't the only one. Just after I had started boarding school, I went for a cigarette one day with the older girl who was meant to be looking after me. There was a 'smokers' tree' situated at the far end of the school, far away from teachers and the prying eyes of Matron. A girl called Jenny Donaldson was there when we arrived. She was a little older than me and quite aggressive. We had met before, but had never really chatted – smoking often bonded girls of different ages but I didn't feel any warmth coming from Jenny.

As soon as we arrived, she started asking me questions, one after the other, almost leaving me no time to answer them.

Do you have any brothers or sisters?
Yes, a big brother.
Is he at the school too?
No.
Where do you live?
Rinteln (it seemed the easiest answer – my parents could be anywhere by now).
What rank and regiment is your dad?
He's in communications.
Are you going home in the holidays or staying here?
I'm staying here.
Do your parents write to you?
No.

Do they visit you?

No.

Do they send you parcels?

No.

Do you miss them? Do you? Do you miss them?

As she threw the questions at me, I started to cry. This was unusual for me as, generally, I tried to show little emotion, but it was almost as if she was leading me down a path of interrogation which would eventually reveal all the things I was trying so hard to hide. The prefect intervened when she saw my tears.

'Stop being so nosey, Jenny,' she said. 'Leave her alone.'

Jenny screwed up her eyes and looked at me even more closely. 'There's something fishy here,' she announced. 'There's something fishy about *her*.'

I looked aghast at her as she uttered those words and I bent down to pick up my bag, planning to go back to school. Jenny grabbed my arm and pulled me up.

'I know,' she hissed. 'I know. IT happened to me too. IT happened to me and you just have to face up to IT. Get on with your life. You can't change anything and you'll get no sympathy here.'

Every time she said 'IT', she nipped me. If she did sense anything in me, a kindred spirit, it didn't bring out any sense of camaraderie. She was looking at me as if I was filth; it was just the sort of look to take me back to how my dad used to look at me too. Maybe she was right, maybe there was something wrong with me – or maybe I reminded her too much of something she was trying to forget.

I ran all the way back to the dorm and threw myself on my bed, shaking.

There were secrets everywhere, and I still wanted to keep mine to myself. I'd decide when to talk – it wouldn't be down to someone like Jenny Donaldson. I'd had enough of bullies to last me a lifetime.

CHAPTER 23

MOVING ON

There were more damaged souls than just me and Jenny. One girl called Hannah, who was almost sixteen, actually ran away during the night. She'd saved up enough money to try and get back to Scotland where her grandparents were. She was caught at the airport. Like me, she was one of the pupils who didn't go home over the holidays. Jodie told me she had seen her in the corridor when she had been brought back. Hannah was shouting and screaming that she refused to go back home, but the matron of her dorm was saying it was her parents' wish and she was to be taken out of school. Hannah was told there was no other way and that her dad would pick her up on the last day of term. She ran away again a few nights before that, but was caught once more – we never saw her again. When the story came out, it spoke volumes to me that she had wanted to get to her grandparents, not her mum and dad.

The other girls would gossip about people like Hannah and what she'd done, but they would talk around what, to me, seemed the real issues. They'd discuss how much money she'd saved, or what time of night she ran away, but it was almost as if they were scared to address the questions which remained unasked. *Why* was she so desperate to avoid going home? *Why* did she cry so much when told she had to be returned to her parents? No one wanted to pick at the seams; who knew how many girls would unravel if that happened?

Instead, we all focused on what every teenage girl found solace in: music and fashion. The 1970s may have been the decade that taste forgot, but when you were living in the middle of it, the sartorial horrors seemed an absolute delight! We lusted after mud-brown culottes and orange wraparound skirts. There was no such thing as 'too much' denim. Bell-bottoms were still around, as were tie-dye T-shirts. Clunky high-heeled platforms were worn with everything, and there were even attempts to hand-make the fashions we saw in magazines. I was never really that fashion conscious, but I joined in as much as I could. Some kids, mainly boys, were even beginning to wear punk outfits, but it was early days and the places they could access such gear were few and far between.

After my disastrous attempt at an Afro hairstyle, my hair grew back, and I was much happier with the next trend – pageboy haircuts. These were, in retrospect, truly hideous. Everyone looked as if their granny had put a bowl on their head and then cut around it, but we all had dreams about sleek, turned-in, mid-length cuts with severe fringes. A lot of girls were also getting their ears pierced – including me.

It was done with a cork and needle, and you simply had to suffer the pain as a rite of passage. We all tried to sneak some big hooped earrings into our daily uniform, but Matron would not allow it. There were notices up all over the dorms saying that only 'sleepers' would be allowed, and we had to abide by it. I was quite grateful. The cork and needle hadn't exactly done a professional job, and the huge hoops dragged my lobes down unbearably. Still, I had a good moan with everyone else about how Frau Schneider simply didn't understand being young.

Music was changing too and a gulf was appearing between the boys and girls as things moved towards the punk years, which would change what we all listened to forever. The girl pupils liked Barbra Streisand, Hot Chocolate and Leo Sayer, we mooned over the Bee Gees and Barry Manilow, while the boys discovered the Sex Pistols and the Jam, Blondie and the Knack.

Over the four years, things did change – not just the outside world and the parts of it which encroached on our lives such as clothes and songs, but what was inside too. It was in some ways an uneventful time in my life, and this suited me fine, but I also changed enormously, gaining an inner strength and confidence I had previously never known I possessed. I kept my head down, worked hard and never really got close to any of the teachers. I had friends, but didn't confide in them; I regret that. I wish I'd told Diana Hayes or Kate everything as I think they would have been tremendously supportive.

As we went through our last year at boarding school, the

dorm girls and I often discussed what we were going to do. The others all planned to go back to their parents and take stock, whereas I wanted to be independent, working and happy. I began to look forward to leaving the past behind me. School had given me four invaluable years of safety and security; from that, for the first time, I was optimistic about my life. At sixteen, my parents would have no hold over me. Although they had shown no interest over the past four years, the thought of legal freedom meant a great deal to me. I could finally become the person I wanted to be.

To get to that point, I would have to see my father again. I knew this was coming but I wasn't as scared as I might have expected to be. I had been away from my whole family for four years, so when I was told I would have to attend a meeting with Dad in the office of the headmistress, I accepted it. This was simply another stage I had to get through to move to the next part of my life.

When I walked in, he was already there. He kept looking at the floor, which meant I could stare as much as I liked. It was odd to see this monster again – and even odder that he seemed so insignificant. I was obviously taller and older, I was a young woman, whereas he seemed to be heading towards old age very quickly. He was actually younger than I am now, but appeared absolutely drained. There was simply no life in him. It was hard to reconcile this *nothing* of a man with the creature who had terrorised me.

The headmistress, Miss Thorne, had to do most of the talking. She made a little speech about how well I had done, how popular I was, how everyone would miss me, but he didn't respond. Miss Thorne looked at me throughout, smiling in a supportive way, and I did the same back to her.

'Mr Black,' she said, 'perhaps you would like to tell Tracy what her options are now that she is able to leave us?'

He shrugged his shoulders and looked at her, not me. 'She has to go to family – there's some in England or Scotland. Ask her what she wants.'

Scotland held good memories for me so I told Miss Thorne I would like to go there. I wanted to be independent and get a job, I wanted a home of my own – and I wanted to make a family. 'Fine,' Dad said, and left the room.

Miss Thorne looked embarrassed. 'Well, my dear,' she said, 'all I told your father was true. We have loved having you here and we hope you have enjoyed your stay.'

I couldn't even begin to express what being at boarding school had meant to me. Through CO Stewart, the Army had paid for me to live in safety for four years, through every holiday, and with everything I needed. I knew I would never see him again, but I wanted to thank him with all my heart. The Army may have harboured a monster in my father, but they had also saved me from that monster.

'I'm sorry that your father has had to leave,' she continued, 'I'm sure he's very busy.'

'Will I see him again?' I asked.

'Yes ... yes, you will. We have to release you to him when you leave us.'

It wasn't a problem. I had escaped. When he came to collect me on the last day of term, I knew we were going to the airport where I'd fly to Scotland and that would be the start of the next stage of my life.

As soon as we drove through the school gates, he parked in a country lane. Without a word, he put his hand on my throat and pressed really hard, so much so I felt my eyes were going to pop out of my head.

'You evil little fucker,' he snarled. 'You've ruined my fucking life.'

The irony wasn't lost on me.

'Do you know what you've done to me?'

I didn't respond.

'Well, I hope you're satisfied. All I can be glad of is that your mother hates your fucking guts now – you've brought it on yourself.'

That irony wasn't lost on me either.

He released me and started the car up again. The rest of the drive to the airport was mostly in silence apart from him finding comfort in calling me all the usual names. The four years since I had left home must have been hard for him as he'd had no one to throw his foul insults at. I just kept looking out of the window, avoiding his eyes and praying for the journey to end. When we got to the airport, he pulled up right outside the front door, jumped out of his seat, grabbed my luggage from the boot and threw it on the ground. I got out of the car while he was doing this and he got in as soon as he was done. He screeched off without another word or a backward glance.

When I got to Scotland, I stayed with family for a few weeks in a village on the east coast. Uncle Bobby and

Auntie Wilma had no idea what had happened – all they knew was that I had left school and didn't want to stay in Germany. Wilma did query why I had been through an expensive boarding school education (she assumed my dad had paid for it) but wasn't going on to further education. I told her I wanted my independence and she seemed to accept it. I needed to stay with them for a month until my sixteenth birthday, but spent those weeks preparing for leaving to start my life alone. They were nice people but they had a connection with my dad and I didn't want that.

I worked at a local farm, pulling tatties and cleaning the chicken coop, for three weeks. At the same time, I was applying to places for another job. I managed to get a position as a waitress at a hotel in Edinburgh, so travelled in from my relatives' place for a little while. Within days of starting, I met the man who I was to marry – Dan. Dan's Auntie Gloria had a spare room available and I jumped at the chance of renting it. As soon as I turned sixteen, I left my relatives. My new flat was in a place near Leith, which was a bustling area of quite high deprivation a couple of miles from the city centre. I was delighted to have the room, even if it was a bit of a dive, and even happier to have a link with Dan. I'd fallen head over heels in love with him, which wasn't surprising really. I was absolutely desperate for love and normality, and also very deluded to think I would find it with the first boy I met. We married when I was eighteen, a month after his Auntie Gloria died. It was far too soon and the relationship was a long way from perfect. I guess I just wanted someone to take care of me. I hated being on

241

my own, which was odd as I had craved it for years and done perfectly well while at boarding school. It was different being an adult though. All around me, people were in relationships and I was desperate to make a perfect life to prove that my past hadn't damaged me.

When I married Dan, I was very naive despite what I had endured. I had only ever had sexual relationships with my father and his friends, and was a complete novice when it came to navigating adult relationships. I almost dismissed what happened when I was abused as completely distinct from the consensual sex a woman has with her chosen partner, so when Dan and I did sleep together for the first time, it was as if I was a virgin.

As I hadn't been in Scotland for long when we met, I hadn't really established any networks of friends. Dan was close to his mum, an alcoholic, and they were the only people I had much to do with. They obviously had their own friends, but I only had them. I found it hard to break into the closeness they had and was always striving to be who I thought they wanted me to be rather than myself. My friends were Dan's friends and the little life we had in Leith was very claustrophobic.

When I got pregnant, I was still a teenager. Joe's birth was long and difficult, I suspect made even worse by the damage which had been done to me internally through years of abuse. Joe was born with pneumonia and stayed in the maternity hospital for three weeks. I stayed with him all of that time as I had to express breast milk for him. It wasn't what I had expected. When you have a poorly baby, all the dreams and images you associate with motherhood disappear and it is very hard to keep going. I was so focused on Joe but I was also very down. This wasn't what I had dreamed of and I actually felt detached from the baby. I willed him to get better and I did all I could for him, but I didn't feel the surge of maternal adoration I had expected, nor did I know that many women have the same reaction to their own baby, ill or not. It took many months before that bond was established, but I did feel a huge sense of relief when we were finally allowed to take him home.

Dan's mother, Cathy, was an interfering old woman, and she was always nosey about my background. She wanted to know why I wasn't in contact with my parents and I was always worried I would trip myself up on my own lies as I tried to throw her off the scent. However, she was like a dog with a bone. She didn't like me, and I suspect one of the reasons she wanted to find my parents was in the hope that she could persuade them to take me far away from her precious son.

A few days after Joe was born, Cathy sailed into the maternity ward. I could smell the booze on her from a mile away, but she seemed happy today, which was out of character. 'I've got a surprise for you!' she announced. I looked behind her, towards the ward door, and there stood my mum and dad. Cathy was delighted. She had tracked them down somehow and discovered they were living at Redford Barracks. Apparently, they had been back in the UK since 1979 and living in the same city as me for two years. Dad had taken voluntary redundancy due to Mum's health, and they were living on a reduced pension about half an hour from where I stayed. I could hardly believe it. I was feeling awful as it was. I was flooded with post-pregnancy hormones and Joe was still really ill – and now my abuser had turned up with the mother who hated me.

It was difficult to say the least. Naturally, nothing was said – I say 'naturally' because my family was based on lies and secrets. My mum seemed to think she could waltz in and be a granny when she had never proven herself to be a mother in the first place. When I got home with Joe, I found it very hard to work out where I was going with my life. I had thought I knew what I needed to be, the person I needed to grow into becoming, but now I was being thrown back to everything I wanted to escape. I hated Cathy for bringing them into my life.

It affected my marriage as I had never gone into detail with Dan about what had happened to me and he was oblivious to how hard I was finding it to cope. We were arguing a lot and he was violent towards me. When we moved house to the Pilton area of the city, I had hoped it could be a fresh start but nothing changed. I wouldn't let Dad visit but Mum was coming round quite often. I always put a brave face on when I saw her because I wanted her to believe everything was working out for me. It was important for me to make her think I had a happy life, a perfect child, a loving marriage and a man who cared for me. The truth was the return of my father into my life coupled with my so-called marriage and the birth had all taken their toll. I remained disgusted at Dad for what he had done and upset at Mum for never having believed me. I have to admit that I never mentioned the abuse again to Mum at that point because I wanted to have a relationship with her. I was hoping against hope she could show that she loved me after all, but deep down I knew she was only back in my life for Joe.

I was very protective of my baby, never letting him out of my sight, but when he was eight months old, I had to accept that I had post-natal depression. Mum didn't know, as I was still keeping up the pretence of having a great life.

It seemed as if I was never to be free of my past, even now I was a wife and mother, but I knew I would keep fighting while I still had breath left in my body.

CHAPTER 24

STANDING MY GROUND

As time went on, we all tried to muddle along. The post-natal depression faded with the help of medication and I continued trying to be the woman I wanted to be. I had told my mother very early on that under no circumstances would I leave my son in their care. Joe would never be left with my father. She didn't even look shocked when I said that, she merely said, 'If that's what you want.' That response spoke volumes to me. If she had believed in her husband's innocence, she surely would have protested at that point?

Visits to my mother's were nearly always when Dad was working. When she came to my house to visit me, he would drop her off and pick her up without coming into my home. After a few months of my shaky reconciliation with them, he started a job as a security officer, which ensured he was in uniform again – I think that really mattered to him, it gave him an identity. When we did meet, he would avoid conversation and eye contact. Unsurprisingly, seeing him was always a reminder to me of the abuse. It made me feel uncomfortable, sick to the stomach and anxious – the memories of what he had done would seem all too real again.

While Joe was little, I saw them maybe once a fortnight (well, I saw Mum really), and I only ever stayed for a couple of hours. Dad was usually working – I think we all preferred it that way as it saved awkwardness. Not that Mum and I had much to say to each other. It was all centred around Joe and what stage he was at. She never asked me how I was or even commented when I would turn up with bruises or a black eye. I shouldn't have been surprised.

I have wondered about whether my father abused any other children. It may have happened in Germany, it may have happened when I was at boarding school or when I left, but I don't know for sure. Paedophiles don't stop as far as I can tell. They keep going until they get caught or they can't do it any more. I do feel that, even if he did abuse others, I was his main focus. From what I learned about his behaviour once he came to Edinburgh, I don't think he continued as he was acting so erratically that he wouldn't have been capable of maintaining the web of lies required to do anything. When he lived in Edinburgh and then on the outskirts, he was a loner, keeping himself to himself.

My Auntie Fiona, Mum's sister, also lived in the village my parents had moved to and saw him every day. She said he was always quiet; she thought maybe he was missing the Army and not adjusting to civvy life terribly well, and Mum had said the same on more than one occasion. My immediate thought to myself was 'Yes, that would be the case – he doesn't have his "friends" with him.' I know that was very bitter, but I *was* still feeling bitter about the abuse and about him 'getting away' with it.

Mum was ill again. She had been diagnosed properly at last, but her body was rejecting the medication given. She had to have her spleen taken out and was in hospital for a few months. When she was first taken in she suggested that I visit her in the afternoon and Dad would come in for the evening sessions, so we would never bump into each other. That was fine by me, although by then I had another new baby and it was a lot to juggle, but she was in there for so long it meant I didn't see just how ill he was becoming too. When I had visited them at their house, or he dropped her off at mine, I caught glimpses. With this new arrangement, I was seeing less of him. I was however gradually getting snippets from Auntie Fiona. According to her, his behaviour was becoming stranger by the day.

One day, Auntie Fiona came to the hospital just as I was leaving. It was intentional as she wanted to talk to me, but not in front of Mum. She said my father was acting strangely at home and, that morning, she had seen him driving on the wrong side of the road. She was keeping the house tidy for Mum and had gone round that morning and let herself in. Mum had wooden wall panels, the décor of the time, but my father had apparently drilled big holes in the wall; not just one or two but dozens. The house was a complete mess and one bedroom was completely full of toilet rolls he had stolen from his work.

Dad came into the hospital just as Fiona was finishing

telling me all of this – I can only assume he had no concept of time either. He looked almost demonic. His eyes were wide and staring, he was sneering like an idiot, ranting aloud, saying, 'They thought they would catch me, but I fucked them up!'

Auntie Fiona said, 'Who are you talking about, Harry?'

He just said, 'You know, you know who I'm talking about! I couldn't find them in the walls but I know they're there somewhere!'

He kept uttering unintelligible drivel to himself. He didn't acknowledge my presence but, then again, I'm sure he didn't recognise Fiona either. She told me to go and get a doctor as she took him to Mum's ward and sat him down. When I returned to Mum he was dribbling at the mouth and sniggering to himself with his eyes wide. Mum was in a room by herself and he was looking around madly. Fiona told Mum he was a little bit under the weather so she had called for a doctor to look at him. Mum hadn't witnessed the short conversation Fiona had with my father but she saw from looking at him that something was very wrong. She was quite poorly herself and I felt so sorry for her. She didn't say much and just stared at him.

The doctor came and observed Dad for about twenty minutes. I had to go as the baby was getting fractious and I needed to pick up Joe from toddler group. I wasn't really interested in Dad but decided to go back and see my mum again that night as her visit had been interrupted.

I was still shocked when she told me where Dad was – it wasn't the place I'd expected, it was the Royal Edinburgh

Hospital. Despite its name, this wasn't an ordinary general hospital – it was known as one thing by locals: the loony bin.

My mum's response was hardly sympathetic to me or him.

'The doctor sent for an ambulance when you left, he had no choice. You must have known,' she said.

'Known what?' I asked.

'About him – about him being …' she made a twisting gesture at the side of her head. 'Not *right*, there's something not right with your dad.'

She said it in such a matter-of-fact way but, to me, it was a complete revelation. I knew he was a bastard. I knew he was evil. I knew he was a paedophile. But I had always assumed that these were choices he made. I had never, for one moment, suspected he was mentally ill.

When I left Mum's bedside, I went to a café. I needed to be alone and I needed to think. What did this mean? If he was unhinged or mad or had some condition that had always been there, did that mean he wasn't responsible for his actions?

I could hardly bear to think about it as I sat there with a cup of tea getting cold, and the baby asleep in the pushchair.

The same question was going round and round in my head – what did this mean, what did this mean, what did this mean?

Was he absolved of all he had done?

People didn't go into the Royal Ed for fun; in fact, people fought with all they had to avoid the place. If he was in there, it was because there was something terribly wrong, and it was something which had worried medical experts enough to have him detained. I never found out if he had been sectioned, but it was likely. Very few people walked into that place voluntarily. If he was there, it was through necessity, not choice.

I felt nothing for him – in fact I was hoping this breakdown was in some way payback for what he had done to me.

Nothing really happened for about three weeks as Dad needed to be assessed. As my mother was ill, I was able to see his doctor and he explained things to me. He said that he *thought* it was paranoid schizophrenia and they were giving him medication accordingly, which seemed to be helping him. I was told he would have to always take the medication and, as long as he took it, he should be balanced and not suffer psychotic episodes again.

My head was buzzing with questions.

Paranoid schizophrenia was such a major thing and it had brought so many questions to my mind.

'How long has he had this?' I asked.

'I have no idea,' the doctor said. 'It's impossible to know – I'd only be guessing.'

'Then do that,' I urged. 'If that's all there is, do it – guess.'

I needed an answer. Had he suffered from this all through my childhood?

'A number of years,' was all he would say.

'What's the number? How many years?' I probed.

'I really don't know, but probably about ten to fifteen.'

Not long enough.

Not long enough for it to be a valid excuse – not that there could be a valid excuse for what he had done.

The doctor was watching me and now it was his turn to ask the questions.

'Why do you want to know? Why are you so interested in how long he's had it?' he questioned.

I shook my head and didn't reply.

'Is there any particular reason you're asking?' he went on.

I had been insistent in asking my questions, but the doctor turned the tables on me. I wondered whether he knew something, was he prompting me? Perhaps Dad had said things while he had been rambling or perhaps he had talked to someone when lucid; I had no idea but I felt as if I was the one being watched now. My mouth was dry and my heart was pumping but no words came out. I wanted to tell the doctor what had happened but the memory of some of my previous cries for help and the way they had fallen on deaf ears until I found CO Stewart stopped me. Fear of not being believed prevented me from talking – I also didn't want to give my dad an excuse for all the abuse he'd inflicted on me. The very thought of him saying, 'I was ill, I didn't know what I was doing', made me feel sick.

I went back and told Mum what the doctor had said. She asked me if they knew what caused it and I retorted, 'Maybe it's his badness coming out.' She didn't ask me what I meant and only said, 'We all have badness in us.'

I wanted to scream at her – *not when we're five, not when our fathers are raping us and ruining our lives and our futures.*

'Have you spoken to him?' she asked.

'No – and I don't intend to.'

She was ill too, and they had never been close, but I do think she was curious about what was happening to the man she had shared her life with.

Throughout the following weeks, I started having flash-backs. My marriage was crumbling and my husband had proven to be a nasty, violent bully. The boys were taking up so much of my time but I felt I couldn't give them the full attention they needed as I spent so much time at hospital. My dad's hospitalisation and diagnosis had brought back the pain and shame I had experienced and still had to live with. I began to have nightmares again, which I had been free of since my boarding school days. At the time I never believed it was paranoid schizophrenia and I put it down to the guilt of what he had done to me, his own daughter.

One day as I was leaving, Mum said, 'I think it's all down to stress, you know.'

I told her that stress didn't give you paranoid schizo-phrenia but she was adamant.

'I'm sure that's it, Tracy. He never did adjust to life on civvy street – and he had to cope with me being ill for all those years.'

I couldn't help myself from replying, 'Your illness has a lot to answer for.'

'I can't help it, it wasn't my fault,' she said.

'You could have helped some things, Mum, you know that.'

'Let's not go there,' she snapped.

'Let's,' I said, staring her down. I felt guilty because she was my mother and she was in hospital but I could feel the emotion building up and I thought this might be my only chance to say something. 'Let's finally say it. You weren't there and that wasn't your fault. But he used that to get me and when I told you, you didn't listen. Do you know what he did? He raped me, Mum, he raped a child for years.'

'Not this again!' she shouted, and turned away from me. 'I won't hear it! I won't hear another word!'

I left.

There was no point in continuing as I'd never get what I needed.

There was only one confrontation left to have – and the time was coming.

CHAPTER 25

TIME TO FLY

Dad came out of hospital and returned home about the same time as Mum was discharged. While she continued to get better, his state varied. I'm not sure how good he was about taking his medication but, by early summer of 1985, he had been readmitted to the psychiatric hospital. I had spent months in a terrible state. The flashbacks and nightmares were frequent, and the rest of my life was falling apart.

I had to make a choice. I had to decide whether to let this haunt me for the rest of my life or deal with it on my terms.

I opted for the latter – Dad was getting worse and I might regret it forever if I didn't challenge him.

I will never forget that day. I left my children with a friend and took the bus to the hospital. Due to the type of hospital it was, visitors had to be in a large room with other visitors and patients. The staff tended to be in the same room but at a distance. They didn't go in for privacy there as they had no idea how patients were going to be from one minute to the next, but I gave it a shot and tried to position our chairs in a corner.

I asked him how he was and he seemed to be having one of his better days. He was a little distant and almost embarrassed but he always appeared like that around me. There was a long silence – actually, it probably only lasted a minute or two, but it felt like an eternity to me.

How could I start the conversation I had been working up to since I was five years old?

It had to start somewhere.

'Do you remember everything?'

He seemed like such an old man, but he was barely fifty – and he still had the ability to try and avoid responsibility.

'Yes,' he said, 'I took ill and they brought me here.'

'No, I don't mean that – you know I don't. I mean what you did to me when I was little.'

He just stared at me then looked about the room.

'Dad,' I continued, 'I'm asking you – do you remember? You hurt me. I had to be sent away because of what you did.' I said it quietly but I was becoming angry. He began to fidget and squirm like an unruly child getting a telling-off. There was another long silence before he spoke.

'Sorry.'

'Sorry?' I repeated. 'Sorry? So you do remember?'

He nodded very slightly.

'Why then? Why?' I pressed.

'I'm ill, I'm ill, it's my head.'

'That's right, use that as an excuse. I bloody knew you would,' I snapped.

'I'm so sorry, I'm ill, I'm ill, it's my head.' He repeated this a few times and looked quite scared. By this time, he was attracting attention and a nurse came over.

'I'll have to take him to his room,' she said. 'He's terribly upset about something.'

I couldn't speak.

Dad was crying when the nurse took him back to his room. She was trying to calm him down but I couldn't hear anything that was said. After this confrontation I was never left on my own with my father, a member of staff was always present and remained close to him. I was angry, frustrated and emotional. I had waited so long to say that to him – too long. He was in no fit state for me to shout at, he was too confused to make sense. And, I realised, his words were meaningless; for him to say sorry now meant very little.

This was the first time I had challenged him as an adult. Actually, it was the first time I had challenged him at all. When I was little, as time went on, I would fight him, I would say I didn't want what he was forcing me to do, but I had never asked him the questions which now haunted me. *Why? How could you?* Would these questions never be answered?

The next two weeks were a nightmare. I didn't know what to think of myself. Since confronting him, I'd had a real mixture of feelings. I was confused and ashamed that I had, in effect, bullied a dying man. Was I now as bad as him? I felt very low that I had confronted him in such a way, but I also felt he had won and that 'our secret' would die with him. That moment was closer than I expected. I was all over the place – I was glad I had found the strength to do it though. I think people who have survived child abuse as adults – or during it as children – often fantasise about what will happen if and when they confront their abuser. I doubt it ever turns out well – how can it? I'm not sure there was anything my dad could have done to make it better. He had taken too much and he wasn't even the same man any more. What I wanted was to confront the man he used to be, to challenge that man and get some answers. That couldn't happen, which was presumably why I felt so conflicted.

I received a call from my mum to say that Dad had been moved to a medical hospital, the City, as he was complaining of something being wrong with his throat. He felt as if something was stuck in there and he wanted to gag all the time. Again, I thought of the irony.

The doctors at the City examined him and found he had a tumour. He was scheduled for surgery, but when they opened him up they did nothing as he was riddled with it. I remember someone saying to me that he had 'galloping cancer'. Nothing could be done for him. When Mum and I went to see him we were told he was dying by a doctor who took us along to the day room. It was so bad he was only expected to live a few months, but within days he had become much worse and, on the Thursday of that week, we were told he wouldn't last much longer. After we were told, Mum asked me to phone my brother. I knew Gary was in the Army now too, but I hadn't seen him for years.

The person I spoke with in his regiment said they would get in touch with him and he would be given compassionate leave. After I had phoned about my brother, I asked Mum what I should do about Dad's siblings and his mother, my gran. She said she would phone them as it was a time to put old grudges in the past and pull together. She never did.

Most of the time he was doped up for the pain but he did have a few clear moments. On the Friday I was in his room with him on my own, while Mum was outside having a smoke. I saw he was awake and more aware of things. 'Dad,' I said, 'I need you to do something for me. I need you to tell Mum what happened.' I knew he was dying but I wondered whether he was willing to help me get some sort of closure and move forward to a healthier relationship with her. He just stared at me and said nothing.

I lost it at that point. He was slipping so quickly, had become ill so quickly, and I felt my chance was slipping away. I didn't want him to die without trying to explain things, but he was in control as always, even in this condition. I was shouting when Mum came back into the room.

Over and over again, I was saying the same thing: 'Why did you do it? Why did you do it?'

'What on earth is going on?' Mum demanded.

'If you keep denying it, you're making a liar out of me even after all these years!' I shouted. 'You're making her hate me still – wasn't the abuse enough for you?' He'd had his eyes closed throughout it all, but he opened them at that point and looked straight at me. All of my pent-up emotions were flooding out and the tears were flowing down my face.

The Army did me a favour sending me away.

How could you do that to a little girl?

Why did you let your friends abuse me too?

What made you think I was so worthless?

Tell her the truth.

Tell her the truth.

There was so much to get out – I felt as if the clock was ticking and he was going to die before I had a chance to speak. I felt he was silencing me all over again. I told him he had messed up my life and that I hated him.

Mum looked horrified. I'm not surprised – I was horrified at myself. I told her that I only ever wanted him to tell her the truth and we both stared at the old, sick man in the bed.

He said only one word.

'Tracy.'

That was it.

No apology, no explanation, no begging for forgiveness. I walked out of the room.

Mum followed me later and said now was not the time to confront him; I should let him die in peace.

'What about my peace?' I wept. 'When he dies, how will I ever find peace?'

How could anyone answer that?

On the Sunday morning we were told Dad would not live out the day. I had been back to the hospital on the previous two days but hadn't gone in to see him. I'd sat outside the room – I guess I was fulfilling my duties as a daughter without having to look at him. When I was told this was the end, I had to make a decision.

I couldn't leave it. Not for him and not for me. I had to see him again.

I went into the room at midday. I was on my own as I had been for all of my life really.

I would do this, I would stand firm.

I would say goodbye to him in my own way. I would let him know what a bastard he was and that dying was too good for him.

I stormed in, full of righteousness, only to see a shell. He was a sad, frightened, pathetic old man facing death without an ounce of love to guide him through. His eyes were glassy and his skin was like wax. An odd smell came from him and he seemed to be shrinking by the second.

How could this be the human being who had terrorised me for most of my life?

He was nothing.

I thought back over the past. I thought about how he had seemed different in every posting. I thought of how he had led a double life, a hero on one side, a paedophile on the other. I thought of the name-calling, the insults, the beatings. I thought of the medical and physical problems I still had because of what he had done. I thought of the abuse and the rape. I thought of the friends he had sent me to.

I thought of how my mum had never saved me.

I thought of how someone had – of how there had been a

hero, of how CO Stewart had seen it all and rescued me in his own way.

I saw that I had been given a chance. My marriage was a mess, and I knew I had to do something about that (and I would), and my parents would never be what I needed or wanted them to be, but I had what I always had – I had myself and I had hope. If I nursed this bitterness, it would grow. It would consume and ruin me. I had so much of my life ahead of me and I had survived everything so far – why not give myself a chance?

Time was passing and Dad was ready to step away from this life. I would never be able to understand why he did what he did to me but I couldn't be dragged down any more.

'Dad?' I whispered. 'It's over, isn't it? It's all over.'

There was no reaction or response.

I had to do this for me, not for him.

'Dad,' I tried again. 'It's OK, it's done – I'll be fine.'

I don't know if he heard or understood me. I hope so. I hope it stayed with him.

I sat there and just watched him. At 3pm, the doctors said he was going to last only minutes. I touched his hand and it felt right.

'Goodbye, Dad,' I said. 'Goodbye.'

Mum was there by now and I left the room so they could say their goodbyes.

I don't know if dying was peaceful for him.

I hope so.

Gary was too late. When he arrived, he called the hospital to say he was on his way, but Dad had already gone – I would never see or hear from my brother again – he didn't hang around for the funeral. I split up with Dan five months after my dad's death. My mum made a miraculous recovery and was never ill from her condition again – and she remarried. Everyone was moving on and I knew without doubt that I had to as well. Too many people for too many years had taken too much from me.

It was time for the rest of my life to start – it was time for me to fly.

EPILOGUE

SILENT NO MORE

Sometimes I think we are almost immune to child abuse. It has always happened, it has always been there as a dark side of human history, but the telling of abuse survivors' stories is much more public than ever before. This can only be a good thing. When I was little, no one really spoke about it. Now that many brave people have come forward to tell of the horrors inflicted on them, I think some people feel it has gone too far. There are too many stories for them, too many books, too many court cases. The reality is that there are millions of untold tales and that will always be the case. While you read this, children are being abused in every way you wouldn't even want to imagine – is it wrong for them to have a voice when they are older? Some people complain that books such as these are distasteful. I think raping children is distasteful. I think children who have been silenced for years so that adults can wreck their inno-cence with their perversions do not need to be told to keep quiet a moment longer. Their rights were taken from them in their childhood; we should all hang our heads in shame if that is compounded by silencing them as adults too.

What concerns me is that the number of cases of child abuse is now almost overwhelming. The way some deal with this information is to deny it (as happened with many organisations for many years), suggest it's all made up, or become desensitised to it. If you are in any of those categories, please strip back what I have told you to the bare bones of the story. A grown man raped me. That man was my father. I was a tiny girl of five years old when it began. He touched me indecently, he violated me. He made me touch him, he forced himself on me. He had sex with a child. He chose to do all of this, I did not. He threatened, blackmailed and neglected me. How can anyone possibly say any of that is acceptable, or should remain invisible?

Despite how I have occasionally referred to my father in these pages, paedophiles are not monsters, even if what they do is monstrous. It's too easy to describe them that way – I've done it myself, in this book. But actually, they're just men, they're just people, but they're people who damage and ruin the lives of others for their own needs and desires. But they are 'ordinary'. They are fathers and teachers; they are police officers and soldiers. They are wealthy and they are poor. They have normal lives – apart from the fact that they want to abuse children. They don't have 'evil' stamped on their foreheads, they don't carry placards proclaiming what they are. They hide and are hidden. They are among us and they are very, very clever. If my father was active now, he would find it all too easy to locate others of the same persuasion. The internet presents the images and opportunities which men like him and his friends sought so desperately. That he escaped detection for so long is horrific, and I have no idea how many other children were affected by his depravity or that of his friends. Even if no one wanted to think the unthinkable, I find it hard to comprehend that so many other things were not picked up on – teachers, social workers, neighbours all missed so much.

But, of course, it is my mother who must take the blame for having her eyes shut tighter than anyone else. My father chose to do what he did – no one forced him and no one else is to blame for that – but there are others who could have stopped it and did not. It horrifies me that these situations still occur, and that children are still living through nightmares.

It has taken a great deal for me to write this book. I tried on a number of occasions, thought about it for many years, but the time now feels right.

There are so many things I would like people reading this book to think about and I hope you'll forgive me if I take a little time to address that here.

I know some will have picked the book up because they have been through similar things in their childhood. If that is the case, I hope some of what I have said has been of help; while everyone's experience is different, there are also so many similarities in how paedophiles work, and you may very well recognise that in my story. If any of this has acted as a trigger for you, please do seek help and counselling if you feel it is appropriate for you. There are many excellent groups and individuals out there, and it is never too late to try and reclaim some of your past. I myself can offer no special counselling skills, but sometimes all people want is to get things out – if anyone wants to contact me, please do so through the publishers or through the email address at the end of the book.

If you have not been personally touched by child abuse then I hope my story will have opened your eyes to just how easy it is for one person to maintain a shocking hold over a child. Perhaps this will make you more aware, more responsive to any child you suspect may be in need. I hope so.

The horror never really ends, because the abusers take so much more than those instances where the abuse has actually occurred. They take our innocence and they take our memories. Many brave individuals now say they are survivors of abuse, but I'm not sure I feel that way about myself. Yes, I have survived, but it still hurts, I still have flashbacks, and I feel that I've struggled through more than anything else.

When my dad died, I didn't feel as if that was an end to it, because I was still left with so many unanswered questions. The main one he would never – perhaps *could* never – effectively answer was so simple: *why?* The medical explanations I had for his condition only went so far, and I have never known whether his schizophrenia caused him to abuse or whether some remorse within him had actually brought about the illness. Maybe he felt guilty. I hope so – he should have done. When he died, he was just an old man, so ill and so incapable of giving me anything I really needed. I wanted closure and I wanted him to say he was sorry; he didn't give me either of those, so, in effect, he was still calling the shots.

I'm now a grown woman, a mother and a grandmother. I have a good life in the sun, and a partner who loves me dearly. It all helps, as does writing this book, but no one can ever give me back what was taken from me when I was a child. To be able to have a voice now is so precious, and I hope I have helped someone somewhere to realise they were not to blame; they are not the sum total of what was done to them.

Thank you for reading my story – I hope it has helped.

ACKNOWLEDGEMENTS

This book may be my story, but it has taken a lot of people to bring it to this stage. I'd like to thank many individuals, some of whom are nameless, all of whom have been vital to my life at some point.

My father was never a hero, no matter how many lies he told himself, but there are good men out there. The commanding officer who intervened by removing me from my abusers will always be in my thoughts. By giving me a route to freedom, he did more than he could ever have imagined. It is unlikely he will ever read this book, but I hope anyone who has ever done a good deed for a needy child will see, through his example, that the repercussions can be enormous and we should all do what we can, when we can, to the best of our ability.

I've wanted to tell my story for so long, but it was only through Linda Watson-Brown that I finally laid my ghosts to rest. Her expertise and work on this book, from start to finish, has been absolutely brilliant. When revisiting the past, memories can be horrendous – but Linda, through her understanding, patience and compassion, made this journey possible. I do need to retain anonymity for the purposes of this book, but if you contact Linda she will pass on all messages to me.

I'd like to thank my agent Clare Hulton for all her hard work and making it all possible; once she and Linda were involved, I couldn't quite believe how quickly everything happened.

I have had to use a pseudonym for this book in order to protect the identities of some. I have also had to remove some details, and blur other aspects of my story for the same reason. My mother's illness was finally named, but I can't say what it was as the rareness of the condition could lead to identification. The publishers are fully aware of all these points and I'd like to thank them for their understanding and support throughout. Kerri Sharp has been particularly helpful, with both professional and personal matters relating to the book, and I couldn't have wished for a better team at Simon and Schuster. I'd like to thank them, not just for what they've done for me, but also for the fact that, in publishing stories like this, they are raising awareness and helping others who have been through the same. Sadly, there are far too many of us.

I hope there are people reading this who get strength from my tale and who realise they are not alone, no matter what horrors they have lived through or what nightmares they still remember.

You were never in the wrong, you were never the 'bad'

Acknowledgements

one – but you are the person who is still standing and, for that, you should be immensely proud.

If you would like to contact Tracy, please feel free to do so in confidence through Linda Watson-Brown at www.lindawatsonbrown.co.uk